Case Studies of the Superintendency

**Edited by
Paula M. Short and
Jay Paredes Scribner**

A SCARECROWEDUCATION BOOK

The Scarecrow Press, Inc.
Lanham, Maryland, and Oxford
2000

A SCARECROWEDUCATION BOOK

Published in the United States of America
by Scarecrow Press, Inc.
A Member of the Rowman & Littlefield Publishing Group
4720 Boston Way, Lanham, Maryland 20706
www.scarecroweducation.com

12 Hid's Copse Road
Cumnor Hill, Oxford OX2 9JJ, England

British Library Cataloging in Publication Information Available

Library of Congress Cataloging-in-Publication Data
Case studies of the superintency / edited by Paula M. Short and Jay
    Paredes Scribner.
        p.   cm.
    Includes bibliographical references and index.
    ISBN 0-8108-3752-8 (cloth : alk. paper) – ISBN 0-8108-4543-1
    (pbk. : alk. paper)
    1.   School superintendents–United States–Case studies. 2.
School management and organization–United States–Case studies.
    I. Short, Paula M.   II. Scribner, Jay Paredes, 1963- .
    LB2831.72C38 2000
    372.2'.011–dc21
                                                                99-055522

♾™ The paper used in this publication meets the minimum requirements of
American National Standard for Information Sciences—Permanence of
Paper for Printed Library Materials, ANSI/NISO Z39.48–1992.
Manufactured in the United States of America.

Contents

Foreword
Case Studies of the Superintendency

Recently I reviewed job listings and vacancies for school superintendents in major professional journals and print media. As someone who makes his living preparing school leaders, principals and superintendents in particular, I was pleased to see a healthy job market for my students. These ads left me with two other impressions. First, the sheer number of current and projected superintendency vacancies across the United States is staggering. As any school board and educational administration department will tell you, there are currently more leadership positions, especially in the superintendency, than there are highly qualified candidates who want to fill them. The shortage of superintendents in large urban school districts is especially acute. Second, and perhaps not unrelated to the first, is the list of desired qualifications and expectations that these school leaders are asked to bring to the position. In general, school districts are looking for a candidate who is dynamic; confident; visionary; experienced; proactive; articulate and skilled in interpersonal relationships; aggressive; highly motivated; collaborative; effective at problem solving; knowledgeable about instruction, long-range planning, and finance; and able to move districts and schools to the next level of achievement. It is fair to ask, "Where will leaders with these qualifications come from?"

The potential pool of highly qualified candidates is made up of experienced and skilled professional educators who, at various stages in their careers, have met rigorous professional preparation, training, and licensure requirements. This preparation builds on the experiences and skills of aspiring administrators. The challenges and complexities for school leaders at the dawn of a new century lead some policy makers and administrators to look for simple, right answers to vexing problems. In fact, there is a cottage industry of consultants and educational sideshow barkers hawking the latest and greatest models for innovation and school success. What seasoned school leaders know is that there are no silver bullets of technical knowledge or magical models that will solve all of the problems they face in their daily work. What they have learned, through formal preparation, ongoing professional development, and experience, is that effective leadership requires thoughtful consideration and reflection on problems/opportunities in their practice. In this book, Professors Paula M. Short and Jay Paredes Scribner have, together with a who's who of scholars of the superintendency, artfully combined case study methods with problem-based learning on the superintendency. The text provides aspiring and practicing administrators learning opportunities through case study analysis and problem-based learning to build and strengthen the requisite skills for effective school leadership at the beginning of the twenty-first century.

A perennial challenge to university preparation programs is to provide authentic learning opportunities for aspiring superintendents to acquire the professional knowledge, skills, and dispositions to be highly effective school leaders. The primary instructional strategies used in formal preparation programs for training future superintendents include lectures, discussion groups, simulations and role playing, group inquiry, cases studies, and problem-based learning. Though case studies have long been a staple in the instructional repertoire of these training programs, there has not been a collection of cases that adequately deals with the range and depth of intellectual, professional, political, and emotional textures in today's superintendency. Through the use of case studies and problem-based learning, *Case Studies of the Superintendency* provides readers opportunities to draw upon the research and expertise of scholars and practitioners of the superintendency. Each chapter is a compelling narrative that presents realistic and contextually rich cases that call for careful critique and thoughtful problem solving. Each of the ten cases calls for the reader to integrate professional knowledge, skills, and dispositions in ways that strengthen individual capacities to be effective superintendents. The authors of this book have made an important contribution to the preparation, training, orientation, and ongoing professional development of school superintendents. Earlier I posed the question "Where will leaders with these qualifications come from?" Preparing a pool of highly qualified pool candidates to fill increasing numbers of superintendent vacancies across the country calls for collaborative and deliberate efforts by policy makers, university professors, practicing administrators, and school boards to work together. In addition, providing ongoing support and professional development opportunities for practicing superintendents is an equally important aspect of this collaborative work. Professors Short and Scribner and the authors of the cases that follow have demonstrated their commitment to this important work.

Paul V. Bredeson
Professor
University of Wisconsin–Madison

1

Introduction

Paula M. Short and Jay Paredes Scribner

THE LANDSCAPE OF THE SUPERINTENDENCY

The role of the school superintendent has evolved into one of the most complex leadership positions seen today. The superintendent is expected to work effectively with the multiple stakeholder forces that permeate a community. The superintendent must be responsive to political forces as well as a board of education who determines whether the superintendent enjoys a long tenure in a particular district. In addition, the superintendent is expected to run an efficient and effective organization composed of multiple building level organizations occupied by students, teachers, and administrators. Above all, the superintendent is ultimately responsible for improving student achievement and learning—a daunting task for someone removed from the direct teaching and learning process.

Today's superintendent is faced with dueling conflicts at almost every turn. Carter and Cunningham (1997) talk about the opposing forces always at play in the life of the superintendent. This very prominent position is a lighting rod for frustration with public officials and institutions (Mayo, 1999); the current focus on educational standards and accountability illustrates the growing general concern with the quality of schools, teachers, and school leaders. The explosion of charter schools nationally also illustrates the nation's belief that public schools are not meeting educational needs. Report after report decries declining test scores and the general dissatisfaction with how public schools are performing, placing superintendents in the role of defender and protector at the center of this heated conflict over public education effectiveness. The pressures increase and the conflict continues.

Superintendents today must also be transformational and instructional leaders (Brunner, 1998), capable of building collaborative models for decision making. They must negotiate their roles with the board of education as well as find ways to establish productive relationships with boards, teacher unions, public media, parents, business partners, and legislative bodies (Eadie, 1998). While job security lessens as the tenure of superintendents continues to shorten, superintendents must exhibit strong skills in communication, public relations, organization and business/fiscal management, use of technology, strategic planning, problem solving, and consensus building just to survive (Sharp & Walter, 1998).

Confounding these issues are the fact that superintendents who desire to be leaders rarely find clear directions from their constituencies about what they should do or what their constituencies expect of them (Johnson, 1997) and the obstacles facing women who aspire to superintendent positions. Tallerico and Burstyn (1996) explain that women tend to occupy superintendent positions in the smallest, least cosmopolitan districts with the fewest central office administrators and declining enrollments. These superintendents also report more job stress, less satisfaction, and the greatest susceptibility to school board conflict that ultimately results in firings (Tallerico & Burstyn, 1996).

The bottom line is that the role of school superintendency is a tough, complex, but critically important leadership position.

RATIONAL FOR CASE STUDIES ON THE SUPERINTENDENCY

The complex role of the superintendency requires preparation that can provide aspiring school leaders with the opportunity to explore and analyze real-world dilemmas. Case studies focused on the superintendency can give the student an "eye" into the complexities of the job while in the safe environment of the classroom. In addition, cases provide the context for bringing theory into the world of practice in situations that re-create real-world practice and problems (Ashbaugh & Kasten, 1995). Cases bring to life the many and varied situations facing a school superintendent. Cases used in a problem-based learning environment provide optimal opportunity for building skills in problem analysis and problem solving.

There are many case study books focusing on general school leadership or the principalship. However, few—if any—case study books provide a central focus on the role of the superintendent. This case study book intends to partially fill the void in this regard. The role of the superintendent is distinctly different from building-level leadership and requires a special type of case that brings to life situations and dilemmas faced by superintendents in their attempts to provide district-level leadership.

The role of the superintendent has evolved into a complex, critical leadership position. Thus, the preparation of educators for this key leadership role takes on critical importance. This preparation requires strict attention to the complexities of the position and would benefit from the use of case studies focused entirely on the superintendent's role. General leadership cases or cases focused on building-level leadership fall short in providing the needed portrayal of the superintendent's complex role. The cases presented in this book will provide great opportunity to study the role, analyze the tough situations and demands a district leader faces, and, with the problem-based approach, apply theory and best practice to understand and solve a real-life superintendent leadership dilemma.

PROBLEM-BASED LEARNING

Problem-based learning, promoted by the cases included in this book, focuses on authentic problems of professional practice. It is important in that it encourages a collaborative inquiry approach to identify and solve problems of practice. The use of the cases in the preparation of future school superintendents provides experience in dealing with all types of situations that might occur in the role of superintendent.

Unlike the most common form of instruction, the lecture, problem-based learning occurs in small-group formats facilitated by the instructor (Bridges & Hallinger, 1995). It provides the opportunity for collegial approaches to problem solving that increases the students' own skills and knowledge about superintendent leadership. In addition, problem-based learning encourages reflection on action and reflection about action (Short & Rinehart, 1993), in both individual analysis and in-group analysis activities. The modeling of reflective style of thinking is critical to the development of expertise on the part of the future superintendent (Short & Rinehart, 1993).

The problem-based approach presents the student with a significant problem situation in the context of real-world situations with real-world constraints. Students are guided to seek to understand the situation through collaborative analysis of the situation, to search for additional information (literature, theories, data from additional sources) to clarify the problem, and to find alternative solutions to the problem. In many cases, they may be asked to develop a plan for bringing about a solution to the problem. Often, students are required to present the solution as they would actually handle it in the real-life situation, such as preparing and delivering a presentation to a mock school board made up of real school board members.

In problem-based learning using case study situations, the role of the instructor shifts from the traditional role of extensive prior preparation and instructor-led classes to the role of monitor and facilitator. Cases are selected to fit course objectives and often are modified with additions or complicators to fit the specific needs of the course. Instructors must provide the introduction to the case and also the structure of the student teams that will work on the case; as work begins, instructors guide the student teams as they explore, analyze, and problem-solve. As work progresses, it is critical for instructors to have a plan for providing intermittent feedback and ongoing assessment of the teams' progress. This approach allows students to assume a greater responsibility for their learning and forces them into a more active role in their learning experiences as they grapple with solving the problem situation using the provided data and complexities. Cases will vary in their approach to products for the exercise, ranging from presentations to reports often delivered in authentic settings. Such are the cases presented in this book.

THE CASES

Issues facing superintendents now and in the future are well known. Superintendents will have to attend to the needs and desires of increasingly diverse groups, be they students, parents, school board members, or community members. They will have to attend to these groups' needs within the context of legal, legislative, and/or executive mandates, as they are asked to implement a continuous stream of educational reform issues. Each case in the pages that follow touches on several of these pertinent issues. However, while similar overarching challenges facing superintendents are addressed, each case is also unique. We have attempted to summarize these unique characteristics in Table 1.1 by identifying the predominant issues in each case. However, the cases are certainly not limited to these issues. Generally, the cases deal with the superintendent's role vis-à-vis such issues as school-, district-, and state-level policies; school board- and community-superintendent relations; leadership style; superintendent and teacher relations; and women in the superintendency.

In the pages that follow, the reader will find case studies that are wonderfully useful tools for teaching issues of the superintendency. Several factors make the case studies in this text so valuable. Perhaps most important, in many of the situations so richly portrayed in the following chapters, the authors have incorporated their own direct experiences as superintendents. Second, each of the cases is also grounded in research by some of the most respected scholars on the superintendency in this country. This combination of direct, practical knowledge and the knowledge based on rigorous, systematic inquiry makes these cases both pertinent and powerful. Third, the cases focus on issues that are timeless *and* contemporary; for example, new superintendents will always be faced with issues regarding their relations with school boards, principals, teachers, students, parents, and community members. Fourth, these cases are replete with situations that connect in numerous ways with current educational literature, including systemic reform, planning and organizational change, teacher and student accountability, and the role of the media. Finally, these cases, detailed and rich in their description, lend themselves to introducing relatively novice practitioners to future scenarios awaiting them, and challenging experienced practitioners to wrestle with understanding the role of the superintendency—its inherent tensions, promises, and pitfalls.

REVIEW OF CASES

We provided authors with wide latitude in structuring the cases as they saw fit. However, one requirement that we did impose was to develop cases detailed in their

Table 1.1

	Ashbaugh	Berg	Björk	Brunner	Cunningham	Ramirez	Guzmán & Hoyle	Johnson & Holde	Keedy & Mullin	Ortiz & Mend
Politics/policy	✓	✓			✓		✓	✓		✓
School board	✓	✓	✓	✓			✓	✓	✓	✓
Conflict	✓	✓				✓	✓			✓
Change	✓		✓	✓	✓	✓	✓	✓	✓	
Parents/community			✓		✓	✓	✓	✓	✓	
Teachers				✓	✓			✓	✓	
Legal/law										
Accountability	✓	✓	✓	✓	✓	✓	✓		✓	✓
New superintendent	✓	✓	✓		✓	✓	✓	✓	✓	✓
Leadership style	✓			✓			✓			
Planning					✓	✓				
Public relations/media	✓		✓		✓		✓		✓	
Empowerment	✓	✓	✓		✓			✓		
Student performance		✓	✓				✓	✓		
Curriculum				✓						
Women in superintendency				✓						
Urban										✓

description of context, individual personalities, and social dynamics. It is this richness that we believe offers such utility and strength for students of the superintendency, educational leadership, and policy alike.

Carl Ashbaugh's case, "The Superintendent's Role as Instructional Leader," puts the student in the shoes of the superintendent. This case will cause students to reflect on the superintendent's role as it pertains to school board relations and reform issues such as accountability and high stakes testing. Furthermore, these issues will create situations in which students must consider several dynamics simultaneously, including the superintendent's relationship with the school board, parents, and other community members. Finally, students will have to rely on and develop planning skills for implementing changes in school districts.

Judith Berg's case, "The New Superintendent: Challenges at Florence High School," offers students a district-/school-level situation rich with issues of power, leadership style, superintendent and school board relations, and school-level change to consider. Her case study focuses on a superintendent's desire to infuse a new curriculum (interbaccalaureate) into one of the district high schools and deliver it through the formation of site-based teams at the building level. However, the new superintendent's efforts are met with resistance from skeptical teachers and school administrators.

Lars Björk provides students with a historical perspective of a rural (changing to urban) district from 1982 through the late 1990s. He captures the reality that change in complex organizations (such as school districts) occurs on multiple organizational levels and over time. District-level changes are influenced by state reform efforts, which eventually filter down to affect school administrators, teachers, students, and parents in expected and unexpected ways. His case causes the reader to consider the power and implications of past superintendent legacies. Contrary to more frequent accounts of the negative impact of leader succession, this case illustrates how successive leadership with similar visions, complementary (albeit different) styles can lead to creative change in schools. The fruits of this successful string of candidates is manifested in the creation of a new high school with a progressive principal. Björk's case offers much material on such issues as leadership empowerment, education reform, new superintendents, organizational culture, and the tension between progressive ideas and daily realities of teaching, learning, and administration.

Chapter 5, "Faced with a Hostile Press," by Cryss Brunner, focuses in-depth on a web of relationships spun from the interactions between a hostile media source (i.e., a local newspaper) and officials in a large urban district. The relationships primarily focus on the superintendent and the newspaper, but also substantively cause students to consider dynamic relationships among the superintendent, media, school board, community, and district personnel. This case is also unique in that it is grounded in data from Brunner's recent work on women superintendents. This case lays out for the reader both the details of the superintendent's attempts to handle a media source that is openly hostile to the district and the superintendent. In addition to addressing a timely topic, Brunner's case will cause students to grapple with the notion of power and its manifest issues. Finally, while the catalyzing issue is clearly superintendent-media relations, readers will also have to reflect on the tensions the superintendent experiences as she, on the one hand, is engaged with the media and, on the other, attempts to reach her own expectations for addressing student and district needs and community concerns.

Like Brunner, William Cunningham requires students to consider the inevitably political nature of the superintendency. In this case an experienced superintendent, but new to this district, attempts to design and implement a school renewal process at two high schools in a large suburban (inner-core) district. Thus, this case focuses on micropolitical issues embedded in superintendent tasks related to curriculum development and integration and instructional leadership. Complicating matters further, the superintendent must attempt to use his or her leadership style to bridge growing gaps between an increasingly diverse community, a core of resistant teachers accustomed to feelings of powerlessness, a business community pressing for its brand of change, and parents leery of attempts to implement newfangled educational approaches on their children. Finally, Cunningham asks students to develop short- and long-range plans to address these (and other) challenges.

In chapter 7, Nadyne Guzmán and Al Ramirez recount the experiences of a national award–winning superintendent, new to a district situated in a conservative community. While some issues such as organizational change and school community relations surface in this case, it also adds a personal dimension. Guzmán and Ramirez highlight the balance created by the superintendent between his professional life and personal life (including family, physical and emotional health, and spirituality). The authors also provide reflective questions for students to consider.

The driving concern for the superintendent in John Hoyle's chapter is to improve the district's performance on the to state "report card." This case study provides an excellent example of the ripple effect that poor performance on the state report card can cause for a superintendent. For example, a school board representing longtime members of the community *and* new, upwardly mobile arrivals, and a strong and concerned parent group are two groups whose views the superintendent must address. The superintendent in this case takes an approach to change not seen in the other cases by implementing an administrator evaluation model to spur change in administrator practice and consequently student learning.

In chapter 9, Patsy Johnson and Cheryl Holder take perhaps the most school-based focus of any of the cases. Their case focuses on the superintendent's leadership style and use of power through the window of a three-year change process in an elementary school. By focusing on this "school in crisis," the authors cause readers to delve into the interrelationships among the principal, teachers, an outside expert, and community members and then make assertions about the superintendent's role in the events that unfold. Explicit in this case are issues of school change, power, teacher empowerment, and leadership styles of the superintendent and principal.

The case study found in chapter 10 by John Keedy and Ann Mullin takes a longitudinal look from a superintendent's perspective at the strategies involved in creating learning communities at the school level. Keedy and Mullin structure their case around a series of dilemmas that will cause students to think about the choices and challenges facing superintendents even prior to accepting a district level leadership position. The dilemmas focus on the following themes or issues: (1) proactively choosing a district, (2) reconciling the tension between meeting immediate managerial needs and achieving present and future instructional goals, (3) communicating one's message to others, (4) creating professional learning communities, and (5) creating collaborative school cultures. Cross-cutting these dilemmas are issues of leadership, organizational change, school-community relations, and challenges facing new superintendents.

Flora Ortiz and Mary Mend's case study provides students an opportunity to wrestle with ethical, political, legal, and other dimensions of superintendents' work. The case, set in an urban context, focuses squarely on superintendent-board relations. This relationship is characterized by the types of challenges superintendents will inevitably encounter. Namely, the superintendent must work with a board that is split on a critical policy issue. The conflict springs from whether to implement a merit-based, pay-for-performance system for both teachers and staff. Obviously, this contemporary issue is embedded with political, ethical, legal, and ideological issues that surface to varying degrees in the debates over "efficiency and effectiveness" and "teachers as professionals" or "teachers as workers."

REFERENCES

Ashbaugh, C. R., and Kasten, K. L. (1995). *Educational Leadership: Case Studies for Reflective Practice.* New York: Longman.

Bridges, E. M., and Hallinger, P. (1995). *Implementing Problem Based Learning in Leadership Development.* Eugene, OR: Eric Clearinghouse on Educational Management.

Brunner, C. C. (1998). "The New Superintendency Supports an Innovation: Collaborative Decision Making." *Contemporary Education* 69(2): 79–82.

Carter, G. R., and Cunningham, W. G. (1997). *The American School Superintendent: Leading in an Age of Pressure.* San Francisco: Jossey-Bass.

Eadie, D. C. (1998). "Leading for Change." *American School Board Journal* 185(3): 22–25.

Johnson, S. M. (1997). *Leading to Change: The Challenge of the New Superintendency.* San Francisco: Jossey-Bass.

Mayo, R. (1999). "From the Outside In: Additional Conflict for the Public School Superintendent." *Journal of School Leadership* 9(2): 160–179.

Sharp, W. L., and Walter, J. K. (1998). *The School Superintendent: The Profession and the Person.* Lancaster, PA: Technomic.

Short, P. M., and Rinehart, J. S. (1993). "Reflections as a Means of Developing Expertise." *Educational Administration Quarterly* 29(4): 501–521.

Tallerico, M., and Burstyn, J. B. (1996). "Retaining Women in the Superintendency: The Location Matters." *Educational Administration Quarterly* 32(1): 642–664.

2

The Superintendent's Role as Instructional Leader

Carl R. Ashbaugh

Over the past thirty years, the term accountability has gained common usage in the daily lexicon of educators. Certain important changes have occurred in how account-ability is viewed and implemented during this period. Before the 1960s, educational accountability was determined primarily by what could be called system inputs: per-pupil expense levels, teacher-pupil ratios, quantity of instructional resources supplies, number of teachers with advanced degrees, and so on. In the mid-1960s, prompted by the research of James Coleman and federally funded compensatory education programs, accountability began shifting to system outputs. That is, while not ignoring the importance of inputs, accountability gradually was defined primarily in terms of desired or prescribed academic results.

The accountability movement also resulted in identifying those parties respon-sible for attaining the desired outcomes of the educational process. During the past three decades, for example, the locus of instructional accountability moved first from the individual student to classroom teachers, then to include school principals, school superintendents, and finally school governing boards were added. There has been consistent advocacy for school principals to assume the role of instructional leader, but disagreement has persisted as to what an instructional leader actually should do.

Over the years, in light of a growing, changing, and diversified school popula-tion, the school superintendency has also undergone a shift of emphasis vis-à-vis the instructional leadership role. Once able to give most of their attention to building construction, business management, personnel, and publications, superintendents must now focus on the main business of education, instruction. *Accountability,* as the term is used today, refers to the belief that schools should answer to the public for the academic achievement of their students. Accountability becomes operational through the administration of tests that serve as mechanisms to audit the perfor-mance of teachers. It is out of this milieu that superintendents have experienced an

9

expansion of their expected role and scope of accountability. They are now expected to serve a major instructional leadership role, and they share accountability for the results of the instructional process in their districts, whether they implement a highly centralized or decentralized organizational management system.

In recent years, national educational outcomes have been increasingly criticized by consumers and policy makers as inappropriate and failing to meet the demands of a worldwide economy. The call to reform public schooling has become pervasive. As a result of this criticism, state government has assumed a more significant role in prescribing for the local schools a state-approved curriculum, indicating acceptable pupil achievement benchmarks and how these will be measured, identifying who will be held responsible for reaching the goals, and providing rewards for success. This state-level accountability process is typically driven by the establishment of a statewide high-stakes testing program.

Please note that artifacts to this case are available in the appendix.

SETTING THE STAGE

You are the superintendent of the Pineville City Schools. As you drive away from the central office parking lot, you begin reflecting on the frustrating school board meeting just completed.

Last week, the *Times Outlook* newspaper published a report of the district's most recent state test scores taken off the homepage of the state department of education. The scores were based on the percentage of students at or above grade level in reading and math, and Pineville scores were compared with those of the other school systems in the area. The result was that Pineville scores were the lowest of the comparables although its students' scores in the top quartile exceeded those of all the other area systems. It became clear that the board and the community had been embarrassed and were very concerned by the reported scores.

In the "Public Comment" portion of today's board meeting, the president of the local NAACP chapter had asked, "Why do we have so many black students performing below grade level?" This statement touched a collective nerve with school board members who began to offer comments of their own.

Several had voiced concerns over continued "white flight" from Pineville to surrounding school districts. In recent years, new housing developments have moved to the suburban areas of Pineville, attracting primarily middle-class white families. Not only had this move decreased overall enrollment; it also caused the city's racial balance to shift dramatically and threatened the return of a segregated school system. Pineville schools had been working for about twenty-five years under a federal, court-enforced busing plan to desegregate the schools, and school board members were well aware that these population shifts could jeopardize compliance with the federal mandate.

Board chairman Jimmy Schott responded: "Traditionally, we have been the best school system in our area and one of the top systems in the state. Typically, our students outperform students in other states. Our local supplemental property tax provides the extra resources we need to become the best system in the state. As a result, we have programs in place to meet the educational needs of all our students."

"I agree," said member Fred Hoffman, "but the preliminary test scores printed in last week's *Outlook* will place that reputation at risk. After reading those test scores, many in the community will see our school system as ineffective, and more parents will move to other school systems outside Pineville. Let's face it—people see high test scores as evidence of good schools."

"What's more," said member Randy Hanson, "It will become increasingly difficult to attract new businesses to the community with these low scores. We need a plan to address this situation and we need it now."

The discussion continued until chairman Schott brought closure by requesting that the superintendent bring a proposal to the next board meeting that addresses the current achievement scores and outlines plans to improve student achievement across the board. Now, on your way home, you reflect on that assignment.

SUPERINTENDENT'S BACKGROUND

You have been a school superintendent for twelve years, the last three in Pineville Schools. You served previously in two other school districts: a small rural district and a midsized inner-city district. Neither of these districts, however, was as culturally and racially diverse as Pineville. Immediately before coming to Pineville, you worked in another state with high-stakes testing. There you had gained a reputation as a change agent and someone who was expert in instructional accountability. Students at all levels consistently performed well on both national and state tests during your tenure. You prided yourself on being a strong instructional leader.

In your previous assignment, you had successfully implemented site-based management; instituted benchmark testing (testing a specified number of state objectives each quarter in the same format as the cumulative end-of-the-year state tests). You also required the production of a document that aligned the state curriculum, the instructional strategies, activities, and resources, with the various tests used. Staff members were required to produce pacing guides which described exactly what a teacher would teach sequentially during each quarter. You also began an Administrators' Academy to prepare principals to be instructional leaders in their schools.

Since coming to Pineville, however, you have experienced a different challenge. There is a statewide testing and accountability program in its second year of full implementation at the elementary and middle school levels, and when the board hired you they talked about how your previous experience could benefit Pineville. As one of your first actions, you established a structure implementing the concept of site-based management.

Also, last year under your guidance, citizens had voted for a bond issue to replace an outdated high school and repair and renovate the other schools. But until now, most of your ideas and recommendations dealing with instructional matters have either been viewed without enthusiasm or given wait-and-see status.

You have run up against a culture that lives on past school system successes and reputation. There is an "If it ain't broke, don't fix it" mentality among your fellow educators and community members alike. You also have encountered similar hold-over thinking colored by the past among your staff. Historically, there has been competition between Pineville and other area schools, but little attention has been given to monitoring the academic achievement among individual Pineville schools. In the past, students performing poorly on academic tests were ultimately routed to unskilled jobs or dropped out of school. But now, the school board and the community are exerting increasing pressure to improve all students' achievement on the state tests.

HISTORICAL PERSPECTIVE

Pineville, an urban school system, is known for its progressive style of education. Over the past twenty years, however, enrollment has dropped more than one-third because of residential development outside the school district. The board and the administration have struggled to maintain enrollment over the years by offering a variety of unique and high-quality educational programs geared to meet the needs of all students.

There are elementary enrichment programs for high-achieving students. Students scoring above the eighty-fifth percentile on standardized tests in reading and math are eligible for placement in the program. Gifted and talented students scoring about the ninety-fifth percentile are also placed in advanced sections. Middle school students are offered preadvanced placement classes in communication skills, physical science, Algebra I, and geometry. High school students can participate in honors and advanced placement programs. Pineville maintains strong athletic programs that along with the more traditional sports include golf, soccer, swimming, gymnastics, and lacrosse. The district is also known for its award-winning fine arts programs in music and drama.

In fact, the district has deliberately offered programs that surrounding districts did not provide to lure tuition-paying transfer students—especially gifted and high achievers, athletes, and special needs children. This effort, while somewhat successful, has not offset the overall enrollment district decrease. As a result of the selective enrollment decrease, the district's student population has become bimodal, consisting of approximately 45% highly advantaged students, most of whom achieve at or above grade level and another 45% highly disadvantaged students, most of whom achieve below grade level. Overall, approximately 50% of the Pineville students live in subsidized housing or receive Aid to Families with Dependent Children (AFDC). Almost 50% of the total student population receive free or reduced lunch.

THE STATE'S ROLE

This is the second year of a state-mandated initiative called the School Excellence Plan (SEP). According to this legislative enactment, the SEP has three major components: strong accountability, an emphasis on the basics and high educational standards, and a focus on providing school districts with as much local control over their work as possible. During the first year, of SEP all elementary and middle schools in the state established baseline test data. Now, at the end of year 2, test scores will show how well your elementary and middle schools have performed. Next year, high schools will be required to establish baseline data to project their expected growth standards.

The School Excellence Plan forces school systems across the state to achieve expected growth standards for all students, grades 3–12. At least 95% of all eligible students must be tested annually to comply with the legislation, and test results are reported to the public. This information is intended to inform the public about the status of schools and provide decision makers with information for improving pupil achievement throughout the state.

Growth standards are based on students' performance for the previous year. Expected growth is attained if a student's test score shows one year of growth (100%) for one year of schooling. Exemplary growth occurs when a student's test score shows 110% growth for one year of schooling, or when at least 80% of the students in a school perform at or above grade level.

Student performance is reported each year within four achievement-level percentages for a composite of reading, mathematics, and writing. Level I means that students performing at this level do not have sufficient mastery of knowledge and skills in the subject area to be successful at the next grade level. Students performing at Level II demonstrate inconsistent mastery of knowledge and skills in the subject area and are minimally prepared to be successful at the next grade level. Level III students consistently demonstrate mastery of the grade-level subject matter and skills and are well prepared for the next grade level. Finally, students at Level IV consistently perform in a superior manner clearly beyond that required to be proficient at grade-level work.

If less than 50% of the students in any school do not attain at least a Level III status, that particular school is in jeopardy of being identifying as a "low-performing" school. The other criterion for being a low-performing school is if the school in question does not meet its expected growth for that particular school year.

Principals of low-performing schools must be removed from the school and either reassigned or dismissed. An assistance team consisting of practicing and retired teachers, administrators, university personnel, and others selected and trained by the state takes over the operation and management of those schools that need it most. The stated role of state assistance teams is to help schools improve student achievement. Dismissal of teachers and staff may occur if a team finds an employee's performance inadequate on two consecutive evaluations during the school year.

State law provides for the superintendent to be removed if the superintendent fails to cooperate or hinders progress by the assistance team. Also, according to the plan, a superintendent may be removed and replaced by a state-assigned interim superintendent if more than one-half of the schools in the district are identified as "low performing" by the state board of education.

Local school boards are also held accountable. There are provisions for the removal of board members or suspension from their duties in extreme circumstances, such as failing to cooperate with an assigned interim superintendent or otherwise hindering the local district's ability to improve student performance.

All schools achieving either expected or exemplary gain standards will have the opportunity to receive incentive awards. Local schools may opt to use incentive money for something other than direct bonuses if this use is outlined in the School Improvement Plan and voted on as part of the entire plan. Incentive awards are as follows: For schools meeting their expected gain, up to $750 for each certified staff member and up to $375 for each teacher assistant. For schools classified as "exemplary," up to $1,500 for each certified staff member and up to $500 for each teacher assistant.

THE SITUATION

What the local newspaper reported, and what created the heated discussion at the school board meeting, were the preliminary results of Pineville's SEP test scores compared with the scores of other area school districts. When you realized that the reported results would be very controversial, you prepared information to facilitate a discussion at the next school board meeting. You reviewed explanations in the manual provided by the state department of education regarding the meaning of achievement level percentages so that you could respond to questions about the following test results reported for the Pineville elementary and middle schools.

Pineville Schools SEP Test Scores

	Level I	Level II	Level III	Level IV
Elementary Schools:				
Green Valley	15%	37%	36%	12%
Hickory Hill	10%	30%	30%	30%
Clover River	9%	16%	69%	6%
Washington	15%	37%	33%	15%
Rocky Creek	5%	10%	60%	25%
Waterford	22%	26%	31%	21%
Middle Schools:				
Riverview	7%	12%	55%	26%
Central	13%	36%	39%	12%

The fact that two Pineville schools are designated as "low performing" and eligible for "takeover" by state-assigned assistance teams proves to be both an embarrassment and a contentious topic at the board meeting. All in all, the state test data flies in the face of the successful, positive image the community had constructed for Pineville schools over the years.

Board members make it clear that they have never had this problem before. You begin to sense that the board holds you responsible for the school system's shortcomings, although you have been superintendent only three years and the problems obviously have been developing over the last several decades. Furthermore, you recall how your attempts to reform certain instructional practices have been rebuffed.

First, you try offering a modicum of reassurance to board members. You have learned that there are more than 120 low-performing schools statewide, but only thirty-five trained school assistance teams will be available. Even though Pineville has at least three schools that qualify as low performing, many other schools in the state did much worse. You believe that chances are very good that the state will not send an assistance team to Pineville this year.

After a prolonged and heated discussion, the board charges you to come back next month with a comprehensive plan that addresses the poor test scores and is designed to increase student achievement throughout the school system.

The next day a group of parents appears unannounced at the central office to demand an audience with the superintendent. They bring the educational reporter from the local paper with them and the local National Education Association (NEA) Uniserve director. As you to listen the parents, they demand immediate change. The leader of the group says, "The public outcry in our district requires that you do something now! We don't want you to wait until the state takes over our schools." Another parent says, "Our children are not dumb. Someone has not been teaching them what they should be learning. If the principal had paid attention to what the teachers were doing, this never would have happened." Several others voice their concern over lack of high-quality teaching and leadership. It's clear that they place blame for the current situation on the educators and not their children. You listen without interrupting and when the heated comments began to subside, you again reassure the parents that you plan to make changes that will produce positive results. Finally, they leave somewhat mollified but with a "we'll be watching" attitude.

Two weeks before students are scheduled to return to school, your prediction proves incorrect. You receive notice from the State Department of Education that Green Valley and Washington Elementary Schools have been targeted for "takeover" by a state assistance team. The assistance team will be arriving in two days. You are told to remove the two currently assigned principals and replace them with another principal. After making this difficult decision, you schedule a meeting with the faculty, staff, and parents of the two schools.

Neither of these meetings is a pleasant experience. The faculty and the parents are devastated by the news and clearly demoralized. At each session, you introduce the new principal, explain the takeover process as best you can, and indicate that you view this situation as a systemwide failure, not the failure of a single person. Furthermore, you promise to provide whatever support is necessary to turn the two schools around quickly.

Next, you meet with the electronic and print media to explain the school take-over process. Again, you emphasize that Green Valley and Washington schools are reaping the harvest of past practice by the entire school system, not because of some failure by an individual school. You stress that there will be a major emphasis on improving student achievement systemwide, and you encourage the community to rally behind these schools. You are quoted as saying, "Criticism won't help. We need everyone working together if we are to turn our school system around." The media also contact the PTA president of Green Valley who adds her voice to your own. "I have mixed feelings about the review," she says. "It offers a chance for increased assistance and progress. But I fear that it invites criticism of a faculty and a principal I consider to be excellent. I think they have worked very hard to encourage not only students but parents to be involved. They really, really strive to teach."

THE PROBLEM

Again you remember the plan the school board expects from you and realize that it will require the combined efforts of central office staff, as well as building administrators and community leaders. What will be required are major changes in both the culture and educational practice.

To begin the process, you set up a series of brainstorming sessions with key school and community groups. Prior to these meetings, however, you compile some socioeconomic data that compare the two elementary schools to be taken over by state assistance teams with the Pineville system as a whole. You hope these data will shed some light on the current situation.

The percentage of Green Valley students receiving a free or reduced lunch was 71% as compared with almost 50% for the district as a whole. Sixty-five percent of Green Valley families had annual incomes under $25,000 compared with the system's average of 35%. Only 40% of Green Valley students lived with both parents; the systemwide average was 70%. Washington school data was somewhat improved but clearly reached levels above the system averages. Fifty-eight percent of its students received a free or reduced lunch, 52% lived in households with annual incomes below $25,000, and 47% of Washington students lived with both parents. Finally, if one were to identify only the black students at Green Valley and Washington who scored either a Level I or a Level II on the SEP tests, the number would constitute about 70% of the total minority population of Pineville Schools.

Your brainstorming and dialogue sessions each play a key role in shaping the overall plan. Your first meeting with central office administrators and staff seems to provide solid direction. After reviewing the SEP process and the board's expectation, you ask for comments. The assistant superintendent for education services, Francine

Blackstock, argues for taking a long-term perspective but focusing on a student's earliest schooling experience. "Although our students exceed state testing standards at the high school level, they come to us developmentally delayed," she says. "A large number is not ready to learn and we must prepare them to learn at an early age. This means we must put our resources at the front end of our instructional program."

The director of elementary instruction, Patty Linc, agrees. "I've seen positive results when our youngsters participate in the summer library program. Most of them do not have access to books in their homes; they are eager and excited to get a book to take home after they read it to one of the adults working in the program."

Next, Judd Edwards, the district testing coordinator, reports on the system's prekindergarten program. "There is a definite need for additional programs and resources for younger students who come to our system not ready to learn. We currently have twenty-five children on a waiting list for placement into our pre-K program at the elementary schools." He concludes, "Teachers have observed that students placed in the pre-K program come to kindergarten much better prepared to learn than those students not involved in any type of structured learning environment."

After meeting with the central office professionals, you conclude that the best chance for success is to focus on those students who are developmentally delayed at an early age. You advocate that instructional resources should be placed at the "front end" of schooling continuum, which means concentrating on grades K–3. This approach quickly becomes known as "front loading." One way to capture more resources, you decide, is to reduce personnel allotments based on average daily membership (ADM) at the high school and middle school levels and reallocate these as elementary instructional specialists. Furthermore, you decide that the total enrollment in targeted classrooms should not exceed twelve pupils. You also explore the notion of placing all Level I and Level II students for grades K–3, along with needed resources, at one or two sites. Other design features for the plan were discussed including appropriate and aligned content, teaching strategies, assessments, and resources.

The planning session with school administrators began on a rocky note. After you explained what you meant by "front loading," the principals of Green Valley and Washington schools responded negatively. Both said that they didn't want the program because parents would object to the schools being used to house only Level I and Level II students. What this plan would do, they argued, is to concentrate most of the district's minority students at these two schools and the black community would not be receptive to the idea. One of the principals said that this would stimulate the "white flight situation" once again. He reminded all that when housing patterns began changing, parents took their children to other schools outside the Pineville system. Changing school assignments, he argued, would have the same effect. After much discussion, and failing to come up with a better plan to improve student achievement, the building administrators, by consensus, agreed to support the front-loading concept along with the allocation of additional district resources.

Armed with support obtained from central office staff and building administrators, you schedule three community meetings. The first is held at Calvary Baptist Church. At the meeting ministers question how the self-esteem of black children would be affected if most of them were placed in one or two schools. An NAACP representative remarks that the schools would be viewed as the "dummy schools." A prominent church officer speaks out against the plan, saying, "It sounds like we are headed back to segregated schools." A local black entrepreneur asks, "How do we know that appropriate and sufficient resources will continue to be placed at the front-loaded school? I know your intent is to give the needed resources to Green Valley and Washington but there is no way you can ignore the other elementary schools." During the remainder of the meeting, community members expressed distrust about the idea of front-loaded schools. Some parents were concerned that their children would not understand why they were placed at a front-loaded school or might view their placement as punishment. You are surprised and disappointed with the overall reaction because it appears that members of the black community don't trust you after you have worked hard to include them in the decision-making process.

Expecting the worst, you hold the second meeting at the Central Community Center. Most of those attending are parents of students who would be affected by your plan. The parents are mostly positive about the front-loading concept. One parent states, "This school will help my child. The teachers will be able to help him with his school work and help him catch up." Another parent asks, "If my son performs at grade level by the end of grade 2 or grade 3, will he be allowed to attend his home school or must be remain at Green Valley until he has completed the fifth grade?" A mother stands and when recognized says, "I have four children each at a different grade level. I would have a difficult time getting them to different schools each day." She is supported by a prominent PTA leader who adds, "Parents with more than one child in the school system will have a difficult time balancing transportation, attending parent conferences, school events, and PTA meetings." All in all, the information you get from this second meeting is inconclusive. It's obvious that some members of the community will not support your plan, including some key leaders.

At the same time, many parents were supportive as long as the plan helped their child. Still encouraged by the comments and responses received thus far, you hold the third meeting targeting various civic organizations at the high school auditorium.

First to comment on your plan is the president of the Garden Club. "I'm afraid this situation will become a black/white issue," she exclaimed. A prominent business leader asks, "What resources are provided for our average students? We have given much to our advanced academic programs and our top-achieving students. Now we are proposing to place an enormous amount of resources with our low-achieving students. What are we doing for our average students?" During the remainder of the meeting, comments seem to echo or amplify on those of the first two speakers.

You realize that without broad-based support from all segments of the community, chances for the successful implementation of your plan are slim. Nevertheless, you decide to present the proposal for two front-loaded schools to the school board, along with the negative and positive comments you received at the three community meetings.

After the school board meeting is called to order, chairman Schott asks you to present your proposal for increasing student achievement and improving test scores for the entire system. First, you provide a review of information concerning elementary and middle school students. You especially emphasize the high number of low-performing students at the elementary level and remind the board members that both Washington and Green Valley schools have state assistance teams working in them. You also provide them an overview of the process by which you gathered community input and summarize the comments and reactions received at the three community meetings. You conclude your report by stating, "I'm convinced that if we put all our resources at the K–3 level (front-load), we will improve achievement and test scores. There is some support for placing all low-performing K–3 students in two schools. However, there are those who feel that putting the front-loaded program at two schools will be viewed as a black/white issue."

No sooner are your comments ended when the board's vice chairman, Jamal Hoover, comments, "I cannot support the front loading idea if it means that all our resources are placed at two elementary schools." Chairman Schott agrees. "Pineville Schools have always held high expectations for all students. This proposal needs further study. We should look at other alternatives. The superintendent should present other options to the board at our annual end-of-the-year retreat."

You leave the board meeting frustrated once again. What are the next steps to take? You are convinced that the front-loading concept is workable in some form and will prove successful. But there is obviously some serious resistance to overcome before the system would actually implement such an idea. How will you ever convince the board to buy into your approach? And if you are able to sell some type of front-loading approach, how will its success level be determined? How will the board react if their approved plan is unsuccessful, whatever it proves to be? And how will the community react if we continue to have low-performing schools in the future?

LEARNING OBJECTIVES

1. Acquire an understanding of what the terms *accountability* and *instructional leadership* mean when applied to the position of school superintendent.
2. Obtain insight into the way the role of school superintendent has evolved over time and the implications this change has for preparing to be a superintendent.
3. Gain knowledge about the key ingredients of a high-stakes testing program and what school systems must do to function effectively in this environment.

4. Learn what challenges and conflicts arise when a superintendent is faced with schools that do not measure up to expectations.

GUIDING QUESTIONS

1. If you had been asked to do so, how would you go about assessing the superintendent's plan to decide whether to accept or reject it?
2. Now that the board has rejected the plan the superintendent presented, what will you do to come up with an alternative plan for the end-of-the-year retreat? What will be contained in that plan?
3. Should such things as busing plans, promotion and retention policy, personnel appraisal process, and legal issues become necessary considerations in your planning? Why or why not?
4. Assume that you wish to retain a genuine site-based management structure. How would you do so while exercising your accountability for the overall achievement of students in the district?
5. How can superintendents shape the creation of a positive culture of learning in their community? How would you deal with inaccurate community perceptions of your school system's instructional effectiveness?
6. In what ways do citizens' values affect the student achievement in your school?

REFERENCES

Boyan, N. J. (Ed.). (1988). *Handbook of Research on Educational Administration*. New York: Longman.

Cremin, L. A. (1990). *Popular Education and Its Discontents*. New York: Harper & Row.

Cuban, L. (1988). *The Managerial Imperative and the Practice of Leadership in Schools*. Albany: State University of New York Press.

Elmore, R. (1987). "Reform and the Culture of Authority in Schools." *Educational Administration Quarterly* 23: 60–87.

Fullan, M. (1991). *The New Meaning of Educational Change*. New York: Teachers College Press.

Kirst, M. W. (1984). *Who Controls Our Schools? American Values in Conflict*. New York: Freeman.

———. (1990). *Accountability: Implications for State and Local Policymakers*. Washington, D.C.: Information Services, Office of Educational Research and Improvement.

Lunenburg, F. C., and Ornstein, A. C. (1996). *Educational Administration: Concepts and Practices* (2nd ed.). New York: Longman.

Malen, B., Ogawa, R., and Krany, J. (1989). "What Do We Know about School-based Management? A Case Study of the Literature, a Call for Research." In W. Clune and J. Witte (Eds.), *The Practice of Choice. Decentralization and School Restrictions* (pp. 289–342). Philadelphia: Falmer.

Razik, T. A., and Swanson, A. D. (1995). *Fundamental Concepts of Educational Leadership and Management.* Upper Saddle River, NJ: Prentice Hall.

Smith, S. C., and Piele, P. K. (1997). *School Leadership: Handbook for Excellence* (3rd ed.). University of Oregon: ERIC Clearinghouse on Educational Management.

Tyack, D. B., and Cuban, L. (1995). *Tinkering toward Utopia: A Century of Public School Reform.* Cambridge, MA: Harvard University Press.

Weiss, C. (1993). "Shared Decision Making about What? A Comparison of Schools with and without Teacher Participation." *Teachers College Record* 95: 69–92.

Wiggins, G. (1993). "Assessment: Authenticity, Context, and Validity." *Phi Delta Kappan* 75: 200–214.

3

The New Superintendent: Challenges at Florence High School

Judith H. Berg

The explicit and implicit use of power and how people use it to influence others and to protect themselves is rarely spoken of and difficult to directly observe (Blase, 1991). It is nonetheless ubiquitous in organizations, school organizations not excepted, despite a penchant for political cynicism and naiveté among education professionals. This case makes explicit the necessity for educators to develop political acumen and forthrightly engage in political activities. Although this superintendent is keenly sensitive to the omnipresence of politics in school districts and buildings, he runs into difficulty negotiating cooperation and support. Perceived in his previous position as chief education officer as "intellectual, energetic, but not particularly sociable," he has difficulty establishing rapport and widespread respect. He generally garners early support from those whom he considers intellectual equals. His most ardent and early supporters are parents of gifted children, administrators and teachers who work most closely with him, and frequently board members. Over time, he gains a broader base of respect and even admiration from those who recognize personal and professional benefit from his agenda. Association supporters, the fragile and alienated, and a majority of older faculty tend to undermine his efforts. The current challenge of enhancing an already "excellent" school system is intensely complicated by the reality that this is a "closed and traditional" system in which the laissez-faire style of the previous superintendent is the cultural norm.

THE SCHOOL DISTRICT

Florence School District is located in an inner-ring suburb of a large East Coast city. The community is generally characterized as upper-middle-class professional. While the last decade has witnessed the growth of ethnic diversity, socioeconomically Florence has remained middle-class. Currently, 8% of the student body is African American, 5% are Latino, 2% are Asian, and 1% are classified "other." Thirty eight hundred students are housed in five elementary schools (grades pre-K–6), two junior high schools (grades 7–9), and one high school (grades 10–12). At the district level, in addition to the superintendent, there is an assistant superintendent for personnel and facilities, a business manager, and a special education director. A public relations specialist works part-time out of the central office as well. The director of special education is responsible for programs for the 16% of students identified as "special." In Florence, this includes 5% of the student population formally included in the category of gifted and talented and 11% of students identified by a range of disabilities. The district, noted for its academic excellence, sends approximately 90% of its graduates on to postsecondary education. Although not the state's wealthiest district per capita, Florence has one of the highest per-pupil expenditures in the state. Florence schools are defined by a tradition of "excellence," stability of leadership, and citizen support for its schools. After an arduous selection process, the school board, at the recommendation of its superintendent selection committee, unanimously hired Dr. Jeremiah Snow. He replaced the retiring, thirteen-year veteran superintendent. Snow's charge from the board was to "get us on the charts as one of the ten most highly regarded school districts in the country, so that our students can go to any university they wish."

THE PLAYERS

The Superintendent

Jeremiah Snow is an intellectual. A full head of white hair belies his thirty-nine years but serves well the image he wishes to portray. Raised in a midwestern city, educated in a traditional, highly structured private school environment, Snow had gone on to college and graduate school, earning his doctorate in education, with a concentration in philosophy, in under three years. His dissertation was entitled "The Philosopher as Educator: A Forgotten Era." During those years, he developed a strong interest in educational reform and found himself drawn to concepts of cognition and the creative process. He can quote John Dewey and often does. His hobbies include the voracious reading of military histories and presidential biographies. His slight frame is always urbanely clad, and even in the most trying of circumstances he never appears beleaguered. Professional necessity has made him a student of politics and while no one questions his honesty, he has been characterized as "less than candid." Snow would agree with this description. He is aware the he is often judged as being somewhat autocratic and closed. He would argue that he is in fact open and welcoming of input but that he "does not suffer fools easily."

The position in Florence is Snow's second as superintendent. His previous district, in another state, had a demographic profile similar to that of Florence. Throughout his twelve-year professional career, he has sought out leadership opportunities in districts in which the primary challenge was academic excellence. At age thirty-nine, this would be his second superintendency, and it is especially important to him that he be successful. His first superintendency ended, after a three-year tenure, with somewhat mixed reviews. During those three years he had begun to create a national reputation as a risk taker and futurist—one who helped districts focus on academics. Teachers and administrators concurred that he knew teaching and learning. However, he had resigned his previous position knowing that the board was preparing to request him to step down. Difficulties in his first superintendency grew from what was perceived as "a management style that engenders discomfort." Most significantly, he had enraged an influential segment of the community by "firing" a long-term successful coach. (The reasons were never publicly shared, but the board agreed that Snow had the high ground.) Snow had also divided teacher loyalty when he had influenced the establishment of a hierarchical structure among teachers. This "merit system" included a coveted but divisive "professional teacher" status. Less noticeably contentious but nonetheless difficult, he had, on a divided board vote, influenced the establishment of a limited site-based decision-making model at the school sites. Ultimately, these "negatives" dwarfed his substantial achievements. These included higher acceptance rates for district graduates at prestigious universities and colleges, the creation of faculty forums of inquiry, an editorial position with a reputable academic journal, a highly regarded reputation in the field of staff development, and a Ph.D. earned before his twenty-seventh birthday.

A representative committee of faculty and administrators, including two high school chairmen, comprised the superintendent's hiring team in Florence. They and the board of education were fully aware of Snow's somewhat mixed reputation and hired him for his "skills in moving a district to a higher level of performance." The selection committee's recommendation to the board of education regarding the hiring of Jeremiah Snow was not unanimous. Snow sensed this but, in interviews with the Florence board, felt he was to be offered the superintendency precisely because of his record as an academically focused, visionary change agent, and despite the discomfort his educational decisions sometimes caused. His ability to stimulate meaningful dialogue and generate both excitement and conflict among educators seemed to be exactly what this board felt the district needed. Snow is personally committed to working on being less intimidating.

The Assistant Superintendent

Jimmy Ellison is the "memory" of the Florence School District. At sixty-one, he is the elder statesman in many ways. He is the only certificated employee who has never taught. In fact, Ellison will tell anyone who asks that his interest in car engines and boilers is what got him his first job in the district nearly forty years ago. He evolved somehow into the position as assistant superintendent of personnel and facilities, outlasting nine superintendents. The understanding with each of these individuals was that Ellison took care of the buildings, the buses, the athletic fields, and stayed out of the business of teaching and learning. Once, for a few months, he was acting superintendent. During that brief time, he showed an uncanny ability to hire good people. When the next superintendent came on board, he asked Ellison to continue in that role. The personnel office has been under his direction ever since. The new superintendent, Snow, recognizes his assistant's strengths and recognizes as well the arenas in which Ellison has neither interest nor credibility.

The Director of Special Education

Starting as a teacher of special education, Mimi Sable had earned a reputation as a caring, sympathetic, able individual. She had, on occasions too numerous to recollect, proven an invaluable resource to distraught parents. Through a complex set of circumstances she had gained the ear of the previous superintendent and informally served as his second in command, although teachers recognized her as the "real power in central office." Those whom she supported held her in awe, and this group included the majority of special educators in the district as well as parents of children considered "at risk" or "special." (It was entirely her efforts that brought a gifted program to the district.) Most others hoped to avoid her. Administrators had often crossed swords with Sable when they found their faculties' expectations thwarted by her. Under her direction, Florence Schools had gained a reputation as "the place to educate a child with learning difficulties." In the last four years new student enrollment reflected how widespread this reputation was becoming. Identification of district students as "special," at both ends of that continuum, rose each year.

Although she had not participated on the team that searched for the superintendent, her influence was evident. She gave a favorable nod to the hiring of Jeremiah Snow once she learned of his high expectations. However, in the months since his arrival, they have not "clicked." At the moment, she is harboring a silent furor toward the new superintendent for not including her in the early conversations about the International Baccalaureate (IB) Program. Eventually, Snow learned of her animosity from a new secretary. He is now careful to bring Sable into all substantive discussions.

THE CASE

Snow spent his first six months in Florence observing the district's ways of knowing and doing. He divided his time equally between the district's eight schools and the many other stakeholders in the educational process. He observed and had many conversations. The theme of higher academic expectations emerged as a priority for all board members, a majority of parent groups, and at least four of the eight administrators. Among highly motivated parents it was a persistent and impassioned theme, one he had heard repeatedly during the selection interviews. Elementary teachers were generally not engaged by this agenda. Teacher opinion at the secondary schools was one of mild interest. High school staff recognized that students were achieving acceptable if somewhat uninspired scores on standardized tests and college entrance examinations. Snow noted, however, that neither administrators nor teachers suggested a relationship between curriculum and instruction, and these uninspired outcomes.

The superintendent supports and understands the concept of a district vision and mission and the necessity of assuring that there be a broad base of support for this vision. He anticipates the need to spend time in all of the district's schools with an eye toward achieving this vision. But, by February of his first year, he is certain that initial efforts at improved academic outcomes need to be directed at the high school.

THE FOCUS OF CHANGE

Snow, since his days as an assistant principal in one of Illinois's most prestigious high schools, was a strong proponent of the IB Program, a rigorous preuniversity program that, for many, symbolizes academic excellence and intellectual challenge. Only schools officially approved by the IB Organization* may offer the curriculum. The best and brightest students are paired with the best and brightest teachers. These teachers are trained and certified to teach in the program. Snow hoped they could provide just the focus on academic standards that the rest of Florence High School might emulate. The IB Program, he conjectured, could be the vehicle to jump-start what he sees as a mandate for academic rigor.

THE PROBLEM

While the previous superintendent's leadership style could be characterized as "laissez-faire," this was particularly manifest at the high school. Here there was evidence of a completely hands-off attitude, with nearly total decision-making responsibility left to the principal. During Snow's first six months of observation and questioning, the principal's skills (or lack of them) and the role of high school department chairmen emerged as concerns. (The use of the word *chairmen* is appropriate here as men hold all eight positions.) The superintendent's notion as to what the principal and chairs should be contributing to the education community, specifically regarding the process of curriculum development, instructional supervision, and the development of a rigorous academic program, diverged considerably from the current reality. His concern level rose when he considered that it was to these "leaders" that he hoped to look for support and creativity as the IB program was launched.

*IB is a chartered foundation under Swiss civil code and is a private, nonprofit organization.

In Florence, the position of department "head" was created in 1985 in partial response to the lambasting of the 1983 report *A Nation at Risk*. Eight high school department head positions were created. The understanding was that they were "to bring expertise in their specific content areas." No more specific charge was formally given. In fact, each individual in the chair position, in concert with members of his department, had evolved very similar roles and responsibilities for performance of their nonteaching obligations. Despite an idiosyncratic evolution, each chair currently functions, more or less, as a resource person to department staff. Chairs teach three classes and are charged with performance of department leadership activities for the remaining 40% of their time. The principal specifically holds them responsible for inventory control, budget, coordination of meetings for administrative matters, and the presentation of department concerns to the building leadership team, of which they are members. These administrative functions are widely understood, although there is no formalization of these expectations.

Snow, the district's new chief education officer, believes that the department chair, supervised by the principal, should be charged with providing multiple processes to improve teaching and learning. The implementation of a developmental supervision model, the sharing of information on best practices and research, and the development of formal and informal forums for learning are some of the ideas Snow has in mind. In addition, the superintendent believes that chairs should take responsibility for systematic curriculum evaluation, the results of which are evidenced in a written curriculum. There should be a formalized materials selection process that reflects the department's goal orientation, formal communication processes among department personnel and departments, and establishment of procedures for articulation between and among buildings within the district. His expectations for these men are reflective of those held for him when he served as humanities chair in one of New York State's finest private academies. They were also generally the ones he had held for chairpersons when he was principal of a high school located in a university community in New Jersey. While these efforts had not been universally applauded, they had moved his districts "to the next step" academically. Moreover, these foci are essentially what is demanded when introducing and developing an IB Program. Snow's leadership style is inclined toward supporting the principal as primary facilitator in enabling these expectations to be met.

In October, three months after his arrival in Florence, Snow's assessment of the high school's curricular and instructional program reveals that, all departments at the high school lack articulated, mutually agreed-on goals. Absent, too, are any meaningful supervisory procedures for department chairs or teachers. (A developmental supervisory process was the target of a grievance procedure in 1985 and has been nonexistent ever since.) There is also no systematic evaluation of curriculum, ongoing professional development opportunities, or articulation, either formal or informal, between the two junior high schools and the high school. No department is able to show that instruction is guided by a written curriculum. Junior high–senior high interactions occur minimally and are oriented by the hot-button item of the moment. Most recently, Snow is informed, that involved use of the athletic fields located at the high school. The previous "clash," initiated by the high school mathematics teachers, none too gently accused the junior high school staff of not providing incoming tenth graders with "even the rudimentary skills" necessary for high school success. This latter issue remains unresolved. The agenda for monthly department meetings, set by the chairs, are reputedly focused by discussion of "administrivia," as are most meetings among the principal and his chairmen. The only exception appears to involve repeated discussions concerning the status of negotiations.

The belief that staff development, curriculum development, the establishing of school goals, and frequent, structured articulation with feeder schools can improve teaching and learning is a value closely held by Snow. He believes that these activities will be the responsibility of chairs and the administrative team at the high school. He stresses these values in sessions with the high school administrative team, district administrators and the board. In these meetings there has been much dialogue about infusing these goals into administrators' evaluations. Moreover, Snow has been very clear that at the high school these must also be the evaluation criteria for department chairs. He has the board's strong support, and the verbalized support of Don Emery, the high school principal, although Snow suspects that Emery, beloved of staff and community, does not have the skills to nurture such an effort. The potential for these evaluation criteria becoming an issue with the teacher's negotiating team is also anticipated. This is a contract negotiations year, and the chairmen are classified as teaching staff.

Since late fall, an increase of demands and threats from an influential group of parents who are insisting that their "gifted" students are not receiving a challenging education, particularly at the high school, has been the topic of confidential conversations between several board members and the superintendent. In two instances, he has delicately broached the IB idea. Hearing support in their responses, he initiated similar conversations with the other three board members. Two were very excited by the possibilities. One voiced concern about "elitism" and creating a high school divided by program. Snow assured her that this could be avoided when the IB idea is presented. "Families in this community will choose IB over private education. It gives the gifted and talented another option," Snow reminded her, hitting on the ever present specter of private schooling.

In November, Snow initiated formal and informal conversations with high school personnel. As expected, the IB idea received varying levels of support. While concluding that implementation of these new arrangements would be challenging, with board president encouragement he placed discussion of the issue on the board agenda for public discussion during the last week of January. Parents who were present voiced great enthusiasm. Junior high school staff from both schools were well represented. While acknowledging a potentially valuable experience for some children, they edgily noted concern about the possibility that "the cream will be skimmed from the top of the ninth grade class." High school staff reminded the board that "there are already good programs at the high school that are not IB." Local media, jumping the gun, reported board approval of pursuit of the IB Program and anticipation that it would be implemented the following fall.

FLORENCE HIGH SCHOOL

The high school is home to 1,250 students. Each year, for the past several years, one or two Florence High School seniors have been declared National Merit Winners. Nearly a dozen win finalist status yearly. AP classes, attended by almost 12% of the student body, are offered in all major subject areas. Football and basketball are the major sports, and games attract throngs. A winning debate team, an active play production group, and an award-winning school newspaper (which receives assistance from the public relations guru in the central office) round out the most prominent and popular cocurricular offerings.

Florence High School is typical in both its formal and informal structure. Any sense of "community" that staff may have is exclusively reserved for one's content area. Schedules permit lunch groups to form across department lines, but in general, faculty eat in their department offices. It is here that most of the professional and personal interactions occur. Over the years, one attempt or another at socializing across boundaries has been made. Volleyball games on Friday afternoons, a faculty production of a musical play, secret Santas, and the occasional pro forma holiday parties have all had their day. One or another had been moderately successful; some had been out and out failures with attendance limited to the initiator and friends. Even Principal Emery's efforts to host an end-of-the-year celebration, after several years of modest success, has been abandoned. Only celebrations with winning athletic teams seem to call forth any real camaraderie.

A state mandate to create "site-based improvement teams" (SITs) has brought a rather disparate group to the table in a somewhat routinized manner for the past four and one-half years. Seven teachers from various disciplines, one of the school's guidance counselors, two to four parents (dependent on schedules), two chairmen (the position rotates every other year), the assistant principal, and principal meet monthly. The principal plays the role of affable host, but both agenda setting and facilitation responsibilities are given to Marion Peterson, his assistant principal. Peterson is well organized and efficient, but it is generally agreed that she lacks the ability to "see the bigger picture." She has been Emery's assistant for the past three years. Replacing a crusty old disciplinarian who had been in the position when Emery was named principal, tradition and past practice more or less dictate Peterson 's role. This SIT comes together more regularly than most cross teams at the high school, but they are rather divided over substantive issues. Peterson's style is to let people bring their issues to the table, hash them out with minimal interference, and then take a vote. This frequently leaves several people feeling marginal and on occasion angry. Few stay on the committee longer than their two-year appointment although that option is available. Volunteers for the SIT committee are difficult to find. Usually, the departing member recruits his or her own replacement.

Nearly 25% of the faculty are home grown, having graduated from Florence High School and returning to teach there. Nearly 50% are within six years of possible retirement. Several of the more recent hires come from one or another of the many fine institutions of higher education in the area. These new teachers arrive with trepidation and new ideas, both of which seem to dissipate in short order.

THE HIGH SCHOOL PRINCIPAL

In the two weeks before a formal board vote, the superintendent invested a great deal of time and energy meeting with district administrators and the high school administrative team (consisting of the principal, Don Emery; Marion Peterson, assistant principal; and department chairs). The concept of leadership around issues of teaching and learning, curriculum enhancement, and professional development are not ideas that the chairs reject; however, they convey their sense that it is the responsibility of the principal. Within the week, the superintendent, meeting privately with Emery about his and the board's concerns, is struck again by the discrepancy between his own notions of excellence and those of Emery. Not surprisingly, Emery, with twenty-seven years in the district, seventeen as principal of Florence High School, thinks administrators, teachers, and students work well together, and he unequivocally supports the status quo. He has lived in the district for thirty-two years. He taught PE when he first entered the teaching profession and later taught science as well. His children graduated from the high school, and his son was a star basketball player. He has outlasted several superintendents. As part of the team who selected Snow, he was concerned from the beginning about the superintendent's "track record," especially in regard to athletics. It is known, within a circle of professional intimates at the high school, that while Emery had voiced approval of Snow's hiring as a member of the superintendent selection team, he had done so with reluctance. Snow, too, is aware of this fact. Emery's current plans include possible retirement within two years, and he has cautiously but clearly noted to Snow that the board's growing tendency to be interfering ("Now it's the IB idea; last year it was algebra in ninth grade") figures strongly in his decision.

The superintendent has discerned from multiple sources that Emery is both popular and competent, within the parameters of the previous superintendent's expectations. These competencies include successfully mediating conflict and keeping people at the building level happy and cooperative. The new superintendent is beginning to conclude that his hopes for the high school principal to act as prime mover in a new curricular effort are probably misplaced.

THE DEPARTMENT CHAIRMEN

Recognizing that Emery might not spearhead the reinventing of teaching and learn-ing at the high school, Snow is reluctantly turning his attention to the eight high school department chairmen. His efforts, he now feels, will be directed at creating a team management system, based in collaborative planning and focused by an aca-demic agenda.

The chairs are satisfied with years of autonomy, in both department policy and classroom activity, and distrust the superintendent's agenda. They had learned, even before the superintendent's official arrival in Florence, of an undercurrent of dissat-isfaction among teachers in his previous districts, and this sentiment militated greatly against any of his successes. While it seemed that he had easy rapport with intellec-tual equals, sociability was not his strength. Many of Florence High's more fragile and alienated staff, as well as a number of the older faculty, had already expressed concern to one or another of the chairmen. Snow's frequent presence in the high school, his propensity to enter classrooms and remain for as much as a full class period, had raised many teachers' level of concern. The chairmen are quick to rec-ognize that Snow's interpersonal skills, in spite of glowing recommendations from a number of individuals in his previous district, are not about to win him a lot of friends.

Several discussions with central office staff have convinced the superintendent that department heads will present a united front. In fact, they do just that. To the man they adamantly defended the quality of the content, methods, and standards of ex-cellence that "form the cornerstone of the high school curriculum." In the past, they make it clear, they had been encouraged to make independent and thoughtful deci-sions for their departments. They had done so, they claim, "to the enhancement of their departments and the high school." Proudly, they delineate for the superinten-dent many alumni successes and speak specifically of several graduates who have made names for themselves in one or another pursuit. They suggest that Snow hold a forum with both students and teachers to ascertain the level of "well-being" at their school. Despite some noticeable differences, they present as one. Although he is continuing the conversations, the superintendent is inferring that the majority, and perhaps all, of the department chairs could be unwilling and perhaps unable to per-form to the expectation level he holds.

Chairmen Profiles

Although the chairmen appear to be negative about taking on the responsibili-ties the superintendent hopes to assign them, there are clearly gradations in both willingness and ability among these gentlemen.

Dr. Science is a man whose past commends him to the "halls of greatness" of another era. An earned doctorate in physics from a prestigious university and thirty-one years of teaching have established him as an expert. He was appointed chair of the science department at the inception of the position and has served ever since. His personnel file contains many accolades and positive commendations from parents and students alike. The new superintendent's criteria for acceptable performance are offensive to him. He feels that "this agenda is being imposed by an upstart." He has always enjoyed teaching, especially the order and routine. Professional development, in his opinion, is a waste of resources. "You either know your subject and how to teach it, or you don't" is a statement commonly attributed to him. He is inclined to look favorably on the idea of working with the best students because "today's children come to school with no background." But he feels the IB Program would make demands on him at a point in his career when he is less than anxious to take on new responsibilities. He has, with encouragement from several influential teachers, introduced a grievance proceeding against the superintendent's frequent presence in classrooms and against the establishment of new evaluation standards without a vote by the association membership.

Mr. History is an interesting anomaly. The only chair appointed to the chairmen's ranks by the present superintendent, he is already exhibiting initiative and activity in terms of both supervision and curriculum development. The anomaly lies in the fact that he is also the president of the local teachers' association (the word *union* is avoided). These colleagues consider the assessment of staff, based on a set of "administratively mandated performance criteria," to be "unprofessional." It is only a matter of time before they are likely to urge him to vocalize their opposition to administration. He is the youngest of the chairmen, has taught for eight years, and came to the teaching profession after a brief career in business. In his years at Florence High School, he has earned a reputation as a creative and caring educator.

Mr. English, Mr. Art, and Mr. Mathematics (referred to here collectively as Mr. Eam) all exhibit a "wait and see" attitude. They have, for the fourteen years they each have been in the district, enjoyed the discretionary power they were granted in decision making as it relates to their classrooms. Some have heard Mr. Eam suggest that folks just "wait and he [the superintendent] will be gone; he's never stayed anywhere more than three years," which is, in fact, accurate. As long as Snow is in the superintendent's office, they will make some attempts to meet the criteria as established. While each of these gentlemen may have individual responses to the initiative, for the purposes of this analysis we may regard them as "one." Each has accepted responsibility for one or more cocurricular activity. All are at midpoint in their careers and are acceptably proficient as teachers in their content areas. Students are generally accepting of them, describing each as "OK."

Mr. PE and Mr. Foreign (Language) are nearing retirement although neither has declared his intention to do so. Each is an exceptionally good teacher, and their faculty has long had wonderful role models, although it is doubtful that many are aware of this. Neither man has taken an overt leadership role. They efficiently perform their administrative responsibilities and teach their classes behind the proverbial closed door.

Dr. Technology (previously Mr. Library) has been in the district a year and a half. He is formally one of the chairs although he does not teach classes. His responsibilities, for the one and one-half years he has been in the district, have involved providing workshops in technology, and assessing current levels of technological readiness in the district. On occasion, he works with individual teachers in their classrooms. This occurs primarily at the elementary level. It is understood that he will, at the end of this year, provide the district with a long-range technology plan. While Dr. Technology is located in the high school and evaluated by Don Emery, his charge is districtwide. The recency of his hiring and the limitations on the time he spends at any of the district's nine schools have been barriers to his full acceptance into any one group. His unique span of responsibility mirrors that of only Mimi Sable, the director of special education. Sable, however, is evaluated by the superintendent and is housed at the central office.

A MEETING WITH THE ADMINISTRATIVE TEAM

Jeremiah Snow spent a good deal of time preparing for the February 10 meeting with the high school administrative team. He would present to them the advantages of introducing the IB Program, acknowledge the challenges, and attempt to engage their interest and commitment. He very much hopes that the meeting will end with a plan of action. With this goal in mind, he requested that the principal and two department chairs of Emery's choice visit a school in a nearby city that has successfully integrated IB. Within a week of that visitation, Snow scheduled a half-day meeting with the high school administrative team. This meeting is held in the boardroom, and Mimi Sable is invited to be part of the discussions.

The superintendent allows the social conversation to continue longer than he likes and finally, after a moderately successful stab at humor, begins.

"We are blessed in Florence," he says. "We have a supportive community, good kids, involved parents, and excellent teachers. What we don't have is a vision of what we could be. What I sense is that the district has rested on its laurels for years. And, although these laurels are considerable, we can do more. We owe it to these students, to their parents, and in the end to our community. And it's not only in this room that those sentiments are being voiced. Each of us is aware of the strong push by some members of our parent community to provide more than we currently are for their children. Moreover, the board has declared its interest in doing so and I am personally committed to the IB Program as our best shot for doing just that. I see IB as an excellent chance to meet the needs of lots of folks.

"This is probably redundant for many of you, but I'd like to tell you a bit more about the International Baccalaureate Program and then perhaps Don [Emery], Alan [History], and Carl [Foreign] can tell us what they saw at Boston Academy. I want to go back over it just to be sure we're all on the same page; so please, forgive the repetition here.

"The IB Diploma Program is a preuniversity course of study that meets the needs of highly motivated secondary students. In the words of the founders of the program, it is both 'an idealistic and a practical program' that seeks to provide for the education of the whole person and avoid an overspecialized academic preparation. Students who meet the demands of this program demonstrate a strong commitment to learning and develop the skills and discipline for success in a global world. In addition to the high academic standards, the program aims to foster international understanding and cooperation."

Pausing, he looks around the table. Sable is taking notes. Mr. PE and Mr. Eam are attentive, but their expressions reveal nothing. This is feeling to Snow a bit like a speech, which is not at all conducive to the atmosphere he hopes to create. But he had not been able to think of another succinct way to communicate both his passion for the idea and his commitment to seeing it implemented in Florence. Sipping his coffee, he resumes.

"Although the official curriculum is for eleventh and twelfth graders, the high standards implicit in the IB exams require high levels of preparation at the ninth and tenth grade levels. So we need to be aware that eighth graders will be applying to be part of the program and will leave their respective junior highs to come to the high school. And we need to recognize all the challenges that alone presents. Our application and selection process will need to assure that we choose students with the potential for critical and compassionate thinking—the best and the brightest. After all, these are the youngsters who will go on to Harvard and Yale and Oxford, probably with a year of college courses to their credit. But to accomplish that they have to pass the IB examination in six subject areas, complete an interdisciplinary course in the Theory of Knowledge, and participate in service to the community.

"There are other challenges, of course. Faculty, too, will have to apply to be part of the program. IB teachers are trained in the curriculum, and assessment by IB trainers, and the high school, and the district must be approved as an IB site. As a condition of acceptance, we will, almost immediately, need to choose a coordinator for the program. All of this is demanding. It will require funds beyond those currently allocated to high school programs, and I have the board's assurance that this will be forthcoming. There is, admittedly, the potential for creating a 'school within a school' and all the headaches that can bring. Still, in the end graduates of our IB Program will be prepared for university study. They will have acquired the skills and motivation to be lifelong learners and independent thinkers as well as compassionate contributors to society. Isn't that the very best we could give our kids and our world?

"Enough speech making. I guess it's no secret how I feel about this program and its potential for making us even better than we are. The end result, I hope, is students who know themselves and who aspire to the highest, and a district with a reputation for excellence."

The director of special ed animatedly cries, "Wow, we've got a group of parents who are going to love this." The ensuing silence is broken by the high school principal. Don Emery, glancing at Mr. History and Mr. Foreign for approval, describes their experience during last week's visit to Boston Academy.

"Your description is on target, Jeremiah. It is an incredible program—for certain kids. The teaching environment in those classes is not to be believed. Let me tell you, everyone is paying attention. But I've got lots of concerns. First, it makes traditional programs look like stepsisters. Teachers not in the program talked about feeling 'put down.' Second, IB participation seems to discourage students getting involved in other school activities. They're just too darn busy with reading and writing, I guess. I can't help but worry about the effect on our newspaper and drama programs where most of the high achievers now spend time. And, it's a whole other way of teaching. Interdisciplinary—that's not exactly something we've ever done. It feels kind of elementary.

Emery surreptitiously looks at Dr. Technology, the only one who spent time at the elementary schools. "You know what it's like. The teachers and kids, they sink or swim together."

He paused just long enough for Mr. PE to volunteer, "I hear you Don, but the way I see it, phys ed gets the short straw here. You guys came back from the visit, and I never heard anyone mention the subject. You said they talk about an 'action' orientation, but I don't connect that with what we do. And, don't forget to mention that lesson plans and exams need to be approved by Big Brother somewhere out there in IB land."

Sable shoots him a surprised glance. Mr. Eam's whispered "really" almost goes unheard. Mr. History speaks up softly.

"Our academic productivity is and has always been excellent. The programs we offer serve the children we are educating. Could we do better? Sure, but at what price? This idea is awesome. You would be asking us to be different kinds of teachers and to be responsible for different kinds of outcomes. I'm not about to say that's a negative, but I can't see it happening without a lot of struggling. Come to think of it, I wonder how many of our faculty actually needs to do lesson plans anymore?"

Mr. Foreign, quiet throughout, thoughtfully adds, "I have lots of questions. Mr. History is on target here. Most of our folks probably stopped doing lesson plans a hundred years ago. The kids and teachers at Boston have a whole different look and feel than ours. But there sure was some fancy teaching going on up there."

Mr. Eam and Dr. Technology nod. Dr. Science remains uncommunicative but sour. The superintendent speaks again.

"Gentlemen, Mrs. Sable, I'm not going to say this is simple, but I would suggest that it's worth it. You will see Florence students achieving at levels heretofore unheard of in our district. The school environment will be characterized by academic enthusiasm. We will be valuing learning in ways different from the past. In the true spirit of meeting the needs of all students we will be providing these new opportunities. And we cannot continue to ignore the hopes of the community and the wishes of the board. Our charge today is to find a way to make this happen. We need a high school that students, parents, and employees are proud of, an environment focused by teaching and learning. One way to do that is to create this school within a school as a kind of lab for curriculum development and teaching. Teachers who are nervous about it only need to watch. The group in this room is the one that needs to take charge and move this forward."

Watching the men around the table bristle slightly, it is evident to Snow that he has been a bit insensitive. Quickly he adds, "Yes, lots of good things are already in place, and I don't need to remind you of those. I would not be asking this of you if I did not feel we have an excellent staff and administrators. What I am saying here is that what we have is good but not sufficient. We need a dream. We need to challenge ourselves to do more."

The group takes a break at this point. Sable walks into her office. The superintendent, finding himself at one end of the table while the others gather around the coffeepot, glances down at his notes and walks over to the where the men are gathered.

"You know," Dr. Science is saying, "this is one way to create a really 'white' track. I mean, who do we have now in our AP classes? It'll be even more defined in this IB thing."

Mr. Foreign immediately agrees, adding that, as he sees it, they were going to see a lot more divisiveness in the school. "Students and teachers are really going to be pretty territorial with this. I know how kids on yearbook staff already feel. They certainly don't get the attention the football team gets. But they think they're smarter and get off on that."

"We've been trying to get away from labeling students for years," says the principal. "This is sure not going to help that effort."

Snow decides to leave the room for a bit. Rightly, he senses that they are not going to speak of what their real concerns are while he is in there. Previous experience with the realities of change suggest that beneath all this discussion of what is right or wrong for students, the real concerns are more immediate and personal (Hall & Hord, 1987). He had, in several previous meetings with these men, laid out his expectations for the principal and the chairmen. At those sessions, they had spoken at length of the connection between those job tasks and the IB Program. Those gatherings had evidenced underwhelming support for his ideas, and he could tell that, in the main, they had no substantive knowledge of the practices he was advocating.

The superintendent sits at his desk, thinking of Mimi Sable. She is a quick study and very competent, with a strong and persistent group of followers—a woman, he recognizes, worth having in his corner. He knows, too, that even after seven months of daily contact she has not warmed to him or offered her support. What he suspects is that while she does not want the position itself, the director does want to "play" superintendent from behind the desk she currently occupies.

Silence falls the instant Snow reenters the room. He is consciously controlling intimations of professional frustration. More unusual for him is that he also feels at a loss for words. "I want you to consider next steps," he begins. "Any change is inherently problematic, and processes need to be worked through." He pointedly looks around the table trying to glean what he can from body language. The sight is not a pretty one. All eyes are averted from his, and the silence, once again, is prolonged. Dr. Technology is the first to glance up. The superintendent thinks he notes sympathy. Snow silently counts to himself, trying to judge how long to wait before resuming. But Sable breaks into the silence. Looking directly at the superintendent, she voices the opinion that this is an idea whose time has come. "Parents of high-end kids have been blubbering and sputtering for years. Let's be honest here, shall we." She looks at Don Emery. "Dr. Snow was brought in to make something like this happen, and it seems to me our job is to support him now. Unless you have a better idea, I'd suggest we start talking about who should coordinate this project."

Dr. Science, in the past a frequent target of the director's ire, stares at her. Stonily he says, "Mimi, sounds like you're empire building again. I'm not the least bit convinced that this is the way to go. Where's the evidence that this will work for our kids and teachers?"

Mr. Eam and Mr. PE nod in enthusiastic agreement. Emery placatingly suggests that they need time to "think about this whole thing some more."

For his part, the superintendent considers that they have had ample time to "think." Each individual at the table has been approached either in a one-legged conference or in a more prolonged fashion, about his or her ideas on the IB Program. Back in November, Snow had requested that the principal put IB on all his administrative team agendas and was assured by Emery that this in fact had occurred. When he called today's meeting, he'd tried to convey that the discussion was to be substantive. He was not requesting their approval of the program; he was not even hoping for consensus. Rather, he wanted their input as to how to proceed and some assurance that they would be supportive. Without this support there was little chance this idea would fly with faculty. Jeremiah Snow is now in a quandary as to how to move this group to the next level.

LEARNING ACTIVITIES

Analyzing the Case

Jeremiah Snow's analysis of the situation leads him to believe his next steps must be carefully weighed if he is to get the best response from the administrative group gathered before him. Perhaps his intentions have not been clear, today or earlier. Or perhaps he needs to look beyond this group for leadership and support. He is cognizant of the board's expectations and the cacophony of parent voices. Equally demanding of his attention are the beliefs and attitudes of the leadership team he has assembled. Potentially difficult discussions with the Florence Teachers' Association loom. Another problem is his lack of a professional confidante; Snow is feeling quite isolated and even a bit vulnerable at the moment. He senses his professional reputation is hinged precariously on the successful introduction of the IB program, for which there appears to be little faculty enthusiasm and perhaps even less skill to implement. He knows it would not serve his career to leave Florence (as he would most certainly do within a few years) with the same reputation he earned in his previous district: "cutting-edge thinking, but too tough to work with." Not only does he want to be successful, but he also longs to gain acceptance as a leader with a human side.

Taking into account Snow's aforementioned analysis of the situation (as well as your own assessment), answer the following questions:

1. What is the existing culture at Florence High School? What is Snow attempting to do that is consistent with this culture? What is he trying to do that is contrary to the established culture?
2. Who are the power brokers in the community, school, and district? What is the source of their power?
3. Is there a possibility of building coalitions to support the International Baccalaureate program? If so, which power brokers identified in question 2 need to be part of these coalitions? What will Snow use as "bargaining chips" to encourage their cooperation?
4. Which individuals or groups are likely sources of conflict? How can Snow effectively use this conflict to move his agenda forward?
5. In looking for support, has Snow interacted with all the appropriate stakeholders? If not, whom else might he approach, and how would he persuade them to support the IB program?
6. What are the arguments against this innovation, and who is likely to raise these objections? What counterarguments should Snow provide? (Pay particular attention to the language of persuasion.)
7. As the situation unfolds, what circumstances would force Snow to either abandon or mandate the implementation of the IB program?
8. Considering the issues examined in the previous seven questions, offer your own strategic plan for Snow's next steps.

Extending the Case

1. Upon entering a school system as a new superintendent:
   a. How would you become aware of the existing culture in the district and in a particular school? What actions would you take to reinforce and/or alter that culture?
   b. How would you assess the political landscape, from both a macro- and a microperspective?
   c. How would you begin the process of building coalitions in support of a board-directed innovation that you are hired to implement?
2. Conduct a role play of a school board meeting in which a superintendent is

confronted with a series of questions and diatribe from a group that considers a new innovation to be elitist and discriminatory.

3. Interview several school leaders about their experience in introducing, mandating, and evaluating an innovation that has created significant conflict and dissension. Use the following questions to guide your interviews:

   a. What was the innovation, and why did you embrace it?
   b. What conflict arose, and how did it manifest itself?
   c. What methods of persuasion did you use with those who were opposed? What persuades you that you have been successful with these opponents?
   d. What ethical issues surfaced? How were there issues resolved?
   e. What is the current status of and sentiment toward the innovation? What strategies are you considering for moving the innovation forward?

ACKNOWLEDGMENTS

We would like to extend many thanks to Bruce Barnett and Monte Peterson for their assistance with this case.

REFERENCES

Blase, J. (1991). *The Politics of Life in Schools*. Newbury Park, CA: Sage.
Hall, G. E., and Hord, S. M. (1987). *Change in Schools: Facilitating the Process*. Albany: State University of New York Press.

4

The Transformative Role of School Superintendents: Creating a Community of Learners

Lars G. Björk

The Jessamine County School District in central Kentucky served a primarily rural farming community. Buddy Adams grew up in the county and spent most of his career as a teacher, administrator, and superintendent there. He was a man widely respected as an individual and viewed as a good manager who didn't like to challenge how things were done in the county or in schools. An older resident recalls that it was pretty much "a good old boy" system, and people were generally complacent with how the community and its schools were run. Being adjacent to Lexington, an expanding metropolitan area in Kentucky, the school district experienced steady growth as new people, businesses, and families moved into the county. Many established residents resisted growth preferring to remain a rural, farming community and were content with sending their children to county schools. Since the mid-1960s, the district had experienced remarkable and consistent growth of 150 students per year, transforming it from a rural district of 2,300 students to a suburban district of 6,800 in 1998. Over this period, the expanding student population strained school buildings, budgets, and staff. Although the district had an unquestionable need for new schools to relieve severe overcrowding, administrators underestimated the level of resistance to changes that were occurring until a school bond issue was soundly defeated.

LAYING THE GROUND WORK FOR CHANGE

The Jessamine County School Board had five members. In 1982, a school board election introduced several new members; although they were indistinguishable in many ways from those they defeated in the election, the new members were not aligned with factions that resisted development. They favored the small, rural com-

41

munity orientation. The new school board members included two individuals who worked for IBM, a manager and a plant worker, and a local physician. The physician was subsequently elected chairman and held that position for a number of years. In addition, a local farmer was elected who was outspoken in his opposition to growth and support for no new taxes. The remaining members of the board, however, thought that limited growth was good for the community and the school system. The new school board members reflected a major shift in community attitudes toward change and school improvement. They believed that if growth was to occur, as it had over the past thirty years, the community should manage it rather than allow others to do it for them. These new school board members understood the need to relieve overcrowding in the district and were committed to improving the quality schooling for children in Jessamine County schools. One member said, "We needed to be up to the challenge of being as good as we could be for the sake of the students." They also saw that making these changes would not be easy, and they would not succeed without a strong superintendent who shared their beliefs and commitment to children and learning.

When Buddy Adams retired, the board of education sought out, hired, and then supported a new school superintendent, Don Martin. He was brought into the district from a small independent school district. Administrators described him as being highly intelligent, committed to improving schooling for children, affirming the importance of empowering others, and possessing a good background in finance. School board members saw these as indispensable qualities and necessary for making basic changes in the district. In 1982, one of the first acts as superintendent was to reach out to the community, involve individuals who were the "movers and shakers," and work closely with new board members toward shifting the district's attention to improving the quality of instruction.

He set the stage for reforming the system early in his superintendency by taking steps to relieve overcrowding. He drew up plans for redistricting several schools, putting elementary students on "double sessions," and hiring several new principals. The board adopted these measures, and as one citizen put it, "These things needed to happen." Although these initiatives were not widely popular at the time, they did capture community attention as to the substandard conditions of schools in the district and the critical need for making improvements. The superintendent's knowledge, commitment, and administrative style made these changes possible. Don Martin didn't mind being the "hatchet man" and could "take the heat" when he had to make difficult decisions. As one observer noted, Martin "often moved into the fray with the express purpose of using the situation to make changes." He was the kind of person who saw himself as a change agent and looked for opportunities to improve schools. Another observed, "That may be a key element to changing schools. You need a superintendent with a vision, a commitment to children, and a willingness to take risks. It takes a different kind of person to unstick a district, and it takes a strong board to support a person to make those changes. He understood what it took to make real change happen and never saw himself staying in one place more than four or five years." The board of education that hired and supported the superintendent also knew that if he did what they asked, he probably wouldn't last.

A key element of Martin's efforts to improve the quality of schooling for children was his support for good teachers and administrators in the district. He not only moved some excellent educators into principalships but also identified and empowered strong classroom teachers and central office staff to help lead school improvement efforts. The entire reform enterprise was guided by the board of education's strategic vision of improving opportunities for children to learn. As one observer noted, "The new superintendent came in and basically said that the status quo was not good enough and set the stage for going about making major changes in the schools and the business of learning. He empowered people and then unleashed them." Martin was instrumental in the board of education's adopting a motto included in the district's strategic plan: "Yes we can!"

Martin had a sound understanding of the district's problems and was uncommonly skilled in making projections about the growth of the community and its impact on schools. Over the six-year period that he was superintendent (1983–1989), he was called on to use all of his political acuity in understanding political and policy contexts as well as communicate effectively with a broad array of people in the community to successfully implement needed reforms. Although the board wasn't always unified, he succeeded in working with them crafting a new direction for the district. Making changes was not easy, and some speculated that the more conservative factions in the community were mustering support and preparing to run candidates for the board in the next election. A number of community residents believed they intended to replace Martin as superintendent; however, this did not materialize. He had solid backing from most of the board and was skilled in accommodating differences and persuading the two most conservative members of the wisdom of making needed policy changes. Martin was an individual who derived considerable personal satisfaction in finding and meeting new challenges. As one school administrator put it, "Don was always looking" for his next position. In retrospect, Martin felt that he had accomplished a great deal in relatively short period of time in Jessamine County and that the district's reform agenda was headed in a sound direction. He decided not to remain as superintendent and announced his resignation in January 1989. A superintendent search committee was formed that spring, and Martin left the following June, taking a position in a North Carolina district immersed in school consolidation.

THE KENTUCKY EDUCATIONAL REFORM ACT (KERA)

A challenge to the manner in which Kentucky funded its system of education brought by the Council for Better Education resulted in a decision by Kentucky's Supreme Court declaring the state's entire system of public education unconstitutional. The council, composed of sixty-six property-poor districts, was joined by seven others and twenty-two students and contested funding disparities among all districts in the state. The Kentucky Supreme Court affirmed a ruling made by a lower court in *Rose v. Council for Better Education, Inc.* in July 1989 that struck down Kentucky's system of education as it failed to provide a constitutionally ordered "efficient system throughout the state." This ruling set in motion an unprecedented level of reform in Kentucky. Action by the State Supreme Court compelled the state legislature to systemically and comprehensively redesign its education system. In the spring of 1990, the General Assembly passed the Kentucky Education Reform Act (KERA) that put in place arguably the most far-reaching, research-based outline for educational reform introduced in the United States.

The major thrust of KERA is to improve teaching, learning, and student performance. To accomplish these goals, it institutes high-stakes accountability at the school-level; authorizes school districts to throw out restrictive state curriculum guides and bureaucratic regulations; and empowers teachers through School-Based Decision Making (SBDM) Councils to take responsibility for formulating school policies, defining instructional programs, allocating budget resources, and hiring principals. In this regard, it created opportunities for teachers, parents, and principals at the building level to take greater responsibility for designing and managing instruction, assessing and communicating results to students and parents, evaluating programs, allocating budgets, and providing professional development. These new decision-making and instructional formats captured the essence of systemic reform initiatives in the state. KERA dramatically altered the landscape of education in the state, opening up broad opportunities for introducing innovative practices. Many key provisions of KERA were similar to initiatives launched earlier in Jessamine County and were viewed as highly complementary to efforts directed toward improving schooling.

SUCCESSION AND CONTINUITY

Although the board of education and school-level personnel interviewed a number of superintendent candidates, they couldn't reach unanimous agreement on any one individual until they interviewed Dr. Lois Adams-Rodgers. She was viewed as a person who believed in children, was committed to improving opportunities for students to learn, and regarded empowerment as central to achieving lasting reforms. As one board member put it, "she was also viewed by all of the board members as a person who needed to follow the former superintendent" and provide continuity of efforts needed by the district. As one observer put it, "The status quo had been in place for nearly eighteen years, and during that time, Jessamine County was not known as a stronghold of education or innovation. Then Don came in and turned the apple cart upside down, changed some things, some people lost their jobs, and the district was involved in multiple lawsuits because of personnel actions he took when he came in. In short, it was time to focus on children and build on those changes." Adams-Rodgers was selected to be the new superintendent by a unanimous vote of the board and began her duties in July 1989. "I came to a school district that had a clear focus on quality education, from the board on down," she observed.

The board of education election that preceded Don Martin's leaving the superintendency installed several new school board members. The election, however, didn't dramatically alter the character of the board of education or its commitment to improving education in the community. It remained relatively stable and included the two IBM employees that supported the move to improve the quality of education in the district, a professor from Asbury College, and two conservative farmers. One of the farmers was a woman who had been active in local politics over the past several years. Although both represented a segment of the community very concerned about new growth and taxes, they were staunch supporters of improving the quality education in the community.

When Adams-Rodgers joined the district, she found the system staffed with principals who were regarded as strong administrators, good instructional leaders, committed to improving student learning, and supportive of teacher empowerment initiatives. In addition, she found the central office staff equally competent and committed. Even though some staff had been there for a number of years, they affirmed the importance of maintaining a student-centered approach, supported educational innovation, shared high expectations, and committed their energies to improving education in the district. Adams-Rodgers said, "In schools throughout Jessamine County, principals and staff posted banners with logos and slogans that declared, 'Children Come First.' In fact, we adopted it as a board of education and central office statement of belief."

One of the most important activities underway in the district was formulating a long-range plan. The superintendent recalled, "We continued with the strategic planning process that intentionally sought out and involved different interest groups in the community. The superintendent and members of the board of education became very involved with the county planning and zoning board and helped to anticipate and plan for changes in a reasonable and informed manner." As an influential member of the community observed, "Dr. Adams-Rodgers helped to establish an atmosphere in the community where there was continuing dialogue between the superintendent and shakers and movers in the community." Adams-Rodgers herself candidly reflected, "What I brought to the superintendency was a softer way to keep that communication going."

Her predecessor was able to unstick people from their complacency, get them to believe in themselves, created opportunities for them to do things they didn't think were possible, and when they succeeded, he gave them the recognition they richly deserved. He helped put children at the center of district thinking and action and used this focus as a template for weighing decisions and launching initiatives. He empowered people and then challenged them to make a difference for children. Adams-Rogers observed, "Don Martin created the conditions that made reforms possible, and then I built on that foundation. Everything we did was child centered and based on empowering people to get things done."

She also saw some similarities in her and Martin's leadership styles. "My whole way of leading is through reaching out to people. I can't lead without people behind me, beside me, and sometimes in front of me. I see myself as part of a team." That team approach began with Martin, although his definition of team leadership and Adams-Rodgers's definition were somewhat different. "While he clearly was always going to be captain of the team, I didn't mind and truly valued having a lot of cocaptains."

Adam-Rodgers also connected with people in the community through her involvement as a parent involved in school activities such as band, basketball, and PTA meetings. Parents were very open and talked with her about schools; as a result, she learned a great deal about how parents viewed schools. In addition, Adams-Rodgers was heartened to find a vigorous leadership team in place throughout the district not only in the assistant superintendents, principals, and teachers but in other areas often overlooked, including clerical staff, bus drivers, and food service workers. The district had a large infrastructure with almost 500 certified and classified personnel to support the education of 5,800 students, and many of them understood what the district was trying to accomplish. Throughout the two years she served as superintendent, Adams-Rodgers continued to build the capacity of district staff, empowered them, and used a team leadership approach to improve schools. During the spring of 1991, she accepted an offer by Kentucky's first Commissioner of Education to serve as his chief of staff and joined the Kentucky Department of Education to help implement KERA.

CONTINUITY AND CHANGE

Dr. Larry Allen had distinguished himself as an outstanding educational leader in Kentucky and was hired as Jessamine County's new superintendent in July 1991. His leadership style seemed to combine the most effective elements of previous superintendents in that he related well to the citizens in the rural parts of Jessamine County. He was a good public relations person in the broadest sense. Allen related well with people in the community. As one county resident observed, "He could tell stories, talk about fishing, understood farming." Administrators in the district also appreciated his student-centered approach, commitment to instructional improvement, and beliefs in empowering teachers, principals, and staff to lead district reform initiatives. As Tom Welch, a principal, recalled, "He consistently took the approach that whatever was necessary for children to be successful was what needed to be done. He never gave people the idea that what we were doing was good enough or was working as well as it could. He had a restlessness and an impatience for the status quo because he saw it failing so many individual students all along the way." Teachers and administrators in the district noticed that Allen took the time to make contact with individual students, which added to their respect for him as a caring person genuinely interested in transforming Jessamine County schools.

One of his strengths was his ability to relate to people in rural communities and to explain programs and needs to the board of education. As a result, citizens and members of the board supported district initiatives and committed additional tax dollars needed for implementation. Projecting future district needs, they created a special building fund to support school expansion needs. The assistant superintendent for finance was a native of Jessamine County and a wonderful finance director. He played a major role in helping people understand the financial side of the district's work and, like Allen, was able to communicate clearly why additional resources were needed to respond to the growth and how they would be used. He provided continuity in the district's reform efforts by building upon the solid foundation for instructional improvement laid by his predecessor. The board of education responded positively to his initiatives and enhanced instruction by funding comprehensive staff development programs, and they continued to support peer coaching, additional staff development days for all teachers, the new teacher induction program, and teacher empowerment initiatives started by Don Martin. In addition, they adopted a policy of hiring principals for new schools during the year in which they were built. In this way, principals were involved with the new school from the very beginning and had the responsibility for working with the architect, staffing the school, furnishing it, and serving as its instructional leader. Larry Allen strongly believed in this approach.

WHAT IF SOMEONE SAID YOU COULD HAVE YOUR OWN SCHOOL? NEW-GENERATIONAL THINKING

Understanding outcomes of continuity in the district's commitment to student learning and teacher empowerment may be furthered by observing how the new East Jessamine High School was conceived and founded. The process was grounded in district initiatives set in motion under Don Martin and continued by those who followed his lead. In a very real sense, teachers were encouraged to think about the best of all possible worlds for children and talked openly about "What if someone gave us our own school?" They found themselves in a benevolent environment in which new-generational ideas not only were accepted but encouraged. They were also asked to imagine how they would actually work.

Building the new East Jessamine High School involved a distinct set of political and financial activities. Envisioning what that school looked like, however, involved a remarkably different and creative set of activities. The decision to build a new high school was prompted by the unyielding reality that the Jessamine County High School was built to accommodate no more than 900 students and now housed 1,400. The level of overcrowding was severe, and people in the community knew that something had to be done to alleviate the situation before they could expect to improve teaching and learning in secondary schools. The groundwork for the decision to build a new high school was laid by successive superintendents who diligently worked toward improving relations with members of the board of education and improving communication among the district, parents, and citizens. Resources came from Kentucky School Facilities Construction Commission Funds and the district's bonding capability. Envisioning the core instructional program and creating learning opportunities for students attending the new high school was an uncommon challenge and a rather extraordinary undertaking. Tom Welch was instrumental in working with others in constructing a vision of the new school as a community of learners.

It really started with a telephone conversation in 1993. Welch recalled, "When I was on leave from Jessamine County working as the foreign languages consultant in the Kentucky Department of Education's Division of Curriculum, Dr. Larry Allen, the Jessamine County superintendent of schools, called up and said, 'I'm going to be in Frankfort tomorrow. Can I take you to lunch?' When he arrived, he had a member of the board of education with him. The lunch conversation started to turn toward the district's future plans, and Dr. Allen said, 'You know, we are planning to build a new high school, and we want you to be principal of it.'"

Welch turned down the offer, explaining, "I don't have the certification and I don't have the desire. When I return to the district, I want to stay a teacher." In explaining his position further, he said that since becoming a teacher, "I had a mentor who helped me see that the most important thing that went on in schools was the relationship between students and teachers and that good teachers should stay in the classroom." Welch maintained that perspective, and it didn't surprise his colleagues when he became Kentucky's teacher of the year in 1992. Allen's response to the certification question was "Well, that's all right because we have enough time for you to get your administrator certification by the time we open the school. In fact, we can give you some support when you to go back to the University of Kentucky to get it." He asked Welch to think his offer over and call him later in the week.

Welch walked away from the lunch meeting reflecting on what the superintendent had just told him. He, in effect, really wanted this to be a KERA high school, and he wanted to see how far they could go with the freedoms and opportunities that KERA opened up. In retrospect he thought, "That was very much in sync with what I believe."

Welch reflected on why Allen's offer intrigued him. "In 1989, when I was in France for the summer on a Rockefeller fellowship, I remember getting a letter from Lu Young, a fellow teacher, that kept me up-to date on the things the state legislature was doing to reform education in the Kentucky. It was remarkable! When I got home, I got telephone calls from several other people, and I realized that professionally, as an educator, there was no other place in the country to be than Kentucky. This is where real reform was going to happen." Welch was viewed by his colleagues in school and in the state as a person who was very supportive of children and teachers. After his return from France in 1989, he became heavily involved in KERA and was asked to serve on state-level planning committees.

Welch gained considerable insight into what the state intended to accomplish with KERA while working on curriculum at the Kentucky Department of Education between 1991 and 1994. He was excited about KERA, knowledgeable about it, and intrigued by its potential. In the introduction to *Transformations,* he admonished the "naysayers" and attempted to sway those struggling with KERA implementation by quoting a passage from Antoine de Saint Exupéry's *Little Prince:* "Look in the box and see that everything you need is in there." Before the KERA was widely known or completely understood, people in schools throughout the state called him with questions. A colleague said that during the first years of KERA implementation, "Tom was dubbed 'King KERA.'" Although many people assumed KERA meant "gloom and doom" for education in the state, he saw KERA very differently from most people. Welch commented, "We didn't look at it that way because we had developed professionally in a district that openly encouraged innovation." He saw KERA as having tremendous potential for opening up opportunities for school improvement that hadn't previously existed in Kentucky.

In sum, Welch felt that his beliefs "were in harmony with what the superintendent and board were asking him to do." As he said, "If people who know me and understand that I look at things very differently are still willing to hire me then, let's give it a whirl." He left the Kentucky Department of Education in 1994 and returned to Jessamine County as the director of high school transition, a position that allowed him to oversee construction, program development, and staffing of the new high school.

Welch explained how his unconventional views of schooling had been cultivated over the years. "We developed an idea that was based on an idea of opportunities for kids. We were pushing the limits in our own district with encouragement and support from the superintendent and other administrators for a long time." In reflecting back to the early 1980s and on their work in the district, Welch and Lu Young pointed to the fact that since then the district had a series of superintendents including Don Martin, Lois Adams-Rodgers, and now Larry Allen, who were all very supportive of children. "Children were always the focus, and whatever we could do to make it better for them was encouraged. The reason we look at things so differently is because over the years we were nurtured in an environment that encouraged creativity and to look at things differently. So, we did."

Throughout this ten-year (1988–1998) period, successive superintendents provided the leadership needed to help the board of education see what was good for children and use this as a template for making policy and budget decisions. Members of the board of education were not "micromanagers" but supported these superintendents and allowed them to do what they were hired to do: lead. Members of the board of education were unfailing in their support for the efforts of successive superintendents to improve education in the county. Looking back, Welch and several colleagues noted that these superintendents "empowered others to lead before anybody used that phrase. Not just principals but teachers—anybody who had an idea about improving learning and was student centered."

Beginning with Don Martin, one of the ways superintendents empowered staff was through consistent encouragement to write grants. "He knew the district alone could never supply enough capital to launch the ideas that the teachers had. So, he encouraged principals and teachers to look everywhere they could for grants," Welch explained. During those years, the only district in the state that was getting more grant money was Jefferson County, a large urban school district that encompassed Louisville, which had a population of over one million people. Writing grant proposals helped teachers and administrators to be more reflective about what they did. When they received grant support and implemented their ideas, teaching became more exciting. The more excited teachers became about their work, the more teaching and learning improved. Welch remarked, "We looked in the [Little Prince's] box and saw what was in there and realized that's exactly what KERA was all about!"

The idea of building another high school was not new. It went back six or seven years when Jessamine County Schools went way over capacity. During the 1984–1985 school year, they brought ninth graders to the old high school, which increased enrollment. The old high school had capacity for 900 students; however, after the ninth graders arrived, the school became overcrowded, and the board of education saw that they needed a second high school. When Adams-Rodgers was superintendent (1989–1991) and after Allen began his superintendency in 1991, there was an intense countywide political debate as to whether the county should create a large 2,000-student high school with a big football team or two smaller schools. Most people believed that students would benefit if they knew one another better and leaned toward building two smaller high schools.

Embedded in the debate on size were discussions about what kind of school should be built. One proposal, the "circle document," prepared in 1991–1992 by a focus group that included Tom Welch, was for a pre-K–12 school that reflected KERA thinking and the notion of creating a community of learners. Other proposals included a ninth grade center and a house system. The superintendent, Larry Allen, welcomed this and other proposals and easily entered the flow of these discussions and saw them as an "incredibly fertile ground" of ideas. He was very well read and grounded in research in the field. As one staff member said, "He fostered professionalism by example and often inquired if you had read a particular article or book related to the work in which we were involved. He talked about ideas and brought good speakers into the district. All of that contributed to fostering an atmosphere of professionalism and collegiality." An administrator observed that Allen "had an incredibly creative mind and wanted to explore new possibilities." A high school teacher confirmed this, saying, "He always asked, Why aren't we doing something? rather than Why do we do things? He often floated ideas, got a lot of people involved, formed committees, empowered them, and then listened to what they found." He was very skilled at empowering people, understood the community, and was astute politically. Allen knew what was worth fighting for and understood how to generate board and community support.

As one administrator noted, "'What if' statements often turned into reality because he allowed other people to take ideas and see them through to completion." An assistant principal described him as "having a lot of grit and an individual capable of making difficult decisions. All of his decisions, however, focused on what was best for children and he often sought out more progressive ideas." The decision to establish the East Jessamine High School as a community of learners was a good example. It was preceded by a series of focus groups in the school district and the community; their recommendations were forwarded to the board of education, discussed, and approved. An administrator observed, "By the time it reached them, it was almost a fait accompli. The atmosphere was not contentious, and the decision was made amicably."

Establishing the new high school as a community of learners emerged out of a decade-long intellectual ferment. This different way of thinking about schooling had humble origins. In 1985 a group of high school teachers from the foreign language, science, and English departments housed "out back in the green trailers" at the Jessamine County High School got together around the coffee pot every morning before school. The "breakfast club talked a lot about student learning, what was important, and we were doing a lot of professional reading." As Lu Young observed, "Because a lot of teachers from other disciplines were coming down to our coffee pot, we talked about school. We talked about the idea of having our own school and what it would look like. Then we would go off to teach." As the years passed, teachers continued to read for professional growth, talk about ideas, and ask "what if" questions about how school could be better for children. The breakfast club moved out of the green trailers into the main building, and their talk continued. Starting with the question "What if we had our own school?" led to some interesting conversations.

The breakfast club read seminal works and discussed ideas that fueled their imagination. Young remembered hearing about the work of Willard Daggett and commented, "We were living proof that traditional schooling isn't going to work anymore." Welch added, "Another important work was Jack Foster's *If I Could Make a School* (1991). It underscored the importance of the physical environment in reinforcing the programmatic side of schooling. We also read Sizer's works, but the turning point in our thinking came about serendipitously in 1995 when a fellow airline passenger, a Washington, D.C., consultant, gave me an unpublished, eighty-page manuscript, *Learning on the Edge of Chaos*." Teachers in the breakfast club read through it and began to realize that they were not alone in their thinking about reframing the notion of schooling.

One section described a school, the Illinois Math and Science Academy (IMSA), that was operating in Aurora, Illinois, a suburb of Chicago. Welch called the principal, Stephanie Pace Marshall, and asked whether they could visit the school and talk to staff about their program. Six people, including a member of the board of education, flew up to Chicago and spent a day talking with teachers and administrators in the school. They were very accommodating. The group, however, quickly realized that IMSA was a rather singular situation. It is a residential math and science magnet school for the entire state of Illinois, and SAT scores for their graduating seniors are consistently the highest in the United States.

Although the Illinois Math and Science Program serves a unique population, the visiting team grasped the importance of innovative instructional strategies employed in the program, and they were convinced they would benefit students in Jessamine County regardless of background differences. Young remembered, "We took kernels away with us, lesson plans that helped us think about how to frame significant opportunities for learning. Then we sat down with people in different program areas and talked about what that really meant for children in Jessamine County." Because almost everyone had read Theodore Sizer's works, discussions were substantive and centered on the use of projects, problem-based learning, and exit reviews to assess student proficiencies. Welch observed, "IMSA matched what KERA was trying to do! And it was exactly what we wanted to do in Jessamine County."

There was another consequence of the discussion the group had with Marshall. She asked whether they had read a number of seminal works in the field related to rethinking the notion of leadership and learning. As Welch recounted, "She asked us if we had read *Leadership and the New Science* by Margaret Wheatley. Although we hadn't, we did when we returned home." It proved pivotal in rethinking their notion of schooling and fostered their creative thinking processes about the nature of a community of learners. It was at this juncture that the breakfast club shifted its vocabulary from a "learning community" to a "community of learners."

A "learning community" places primary emphasis on the well-being of the organization as a community, and its activities are focused on accomplishing common, specified goals. In this regard, learning is communal and purposeful. It is not unlike how excellent, traditional schools function. Although individual members are empowered to explore a universe of ideas, these endeavors are intentionally thematic and connected to achieving common organizational goals. For example, a learning community may be viewed as an organization that goes through a double-loop learning cycle. The organization's needs unify community learning, and people are involved in a reiterative cycle of detecting changes in the organization's external environment, aligning activities with new circumstances, learning about how and what was done and altering taken-for-granted beliefs and assumptions. Coalescing the energy of the entire community and focusing it in a particular direction, such as improving student performance, may help an organization respond to demands. Although learning communities represent a clear improvement in making traditional schools more responsive to external demands, it requires considerable organizational resources to orchestrate these activities and achieve optimum performance. Although this is a useful way of thinking about school improvement, according to key members of the breakfast club, it didn't encompass their thinking.

The notion of a "community of learners," however, is next-generational thinking. Owens Saylor, assistant principal at East Jessamine High School, observed,

"Goals are focused on students and teachers, those that inhabit the organization, and relate to enhancing individual opportunities to learn." This intent supersedes goals focused on maintaining the well-being of the organization. As Welch put it, "Individuals in a community of learners buy into goals because of a value and passion for learning shared among every member of the community. That is the strange attractor in a community of learners, and it's powerful." Individuals choose to remain and their efforts are orchestrated, and the organization strives for optimum performance because of shared values and commitment to learning rather than being compelled by the organization to embrace specified, purposeful goals and then coordinating their activities to achieve them.

Welch described it as being a dynamic vortex. It is a vortex similar to a hurricane in that as it spins, it draws energy into itself. In an educational setting, the vortex draws in ideas, human energy, and outside resources. At the same time it is dynamic because, as it spins it is also moving outward, enlarging the scope of learning of individuals within the community. "In a community of learners," Welch explained, "learning doesn't always have to go in the same direction. The breadth of individual exploration and learning are expansive, yet these conspicuously idiosyncratic activities remain in harmony with the strange attractor: a clear focus on expanding opportunities for learning for all students." The superintendent of schools, Larry Allen, was viewed as a member of the community of learners. He had a tag on all his e-mail that said, "Lawrence W. Allen, a learner in the community." Young surmised, "That said a lot. It said that he was open to any experience through which he could learn how to make things better for children in Jessamine County Schools."

Thus, when task forces were formed in 1991 to discuss building a new school, what it would look like, and how it could be different for children, a considerable amount of intellectual ground had been plowed and new ideas were taking root. The ideas that emerged in those meetings were not transplanted or grafted; they were nurtured, tested, and owned by a very wide array of individuals that extended well beyond the breakfast club—the kindred spirits who shared their morning coffee and ideas.

In 1993, by design and agreement, Welch returned to Jessamine County to work with the architects, supervise the construction of the school, and hire staff. "When we began working with the architects, we were able to tell them three things," he said. "First, we wanted the new school to be place where visitors could immediately see excellent student work. We wanted it to be a place where students worked, not where they went to watch adults work. Second, we told the architects that it should be a place where interdisciplinary learning could take place, not just interdisciplinary teaching! Third, we told them we wanted the new school to be a place where there was a sense of flow. Not just a flow of people through wide, well-lighted hallways but a place where ideas and energy could easily circulate." These ideas were not recent discoveries but were gleaned from many years of "what if" discussions about building a new high school. The architects listened to these ideas and used them as a template for designing a structure that complemented new-generational ideas about communities of learners. Although the school was originally planned to open in 1996, construction problems necessitated postponement for a year. The school officially opened during the fall of 1997.

A NEW BEGINNING

Before the first day the new school opened, one of the teachers e-mailed Tom Welch with an uncharacteristically negative message about the awful way the driveways were laid out, warning that traffic into the parking lots would be a disaster. To avoid that, Welch stood at the main entrance to the school directing traffic for the first several days to ensure that traffic moved in the same way around the circular drive. As he recalled, "After three days, things were going wonderfully, and I thought 'That's great!' I have more valuable things to do with my time than stand outside for twenty-five minutes every morning to direct traffic."

However, quite a few parents and students came by and asked, "Did you see me wave at you this morning, Mr. Welch?" or "I was really glad to see you this morning." As Welch recalled, "I suddenly realized that perhaps I didn't have anything more valuable to do with my time between 7:20 and 7:40 A.M. every day than stand out in front of the school." That insight proved invaluable. Every day he waved at students and parents, and students and parents waved at him. They often stopped to talk about their concerns, share ideas, or just visit. When the weather turned cold, some parents would roll down their car windows to tell him to put his gloves on or, when it was snowing, to wear a hat. At Christmas, one parent even bought him a scarf that went with his winter coat! Welch reflected, "These occasions not only reinforce the responsibility I feel for their children but underscore the importance of relationships in creating and reinforcing a sense of community among parents, students, teachers, and administrators." Building those relationships is key to the success of East Jessamine High School as a community of learners.

The notion of creating a strong sense of community and building relations among people was central to the success of new-generation thinking about school. After he was named principal, Welch started talking about the idea of a community of learners. He described it as being different than the traditional model in place at Jessamine High School (which later would be named West Jessamine High School) and explained what the school would look like and that teachers would work in unconventional yet highly effective ways. He spoke at faculty meetings and talked with individuals informally well in advance of October 1996 when they had to make a final decision and declare a school preference. In one instance, Welch and the principal of the "old" West Jessamine County High School presented their individual views on education and then opened the floor to faculty questions. The questions ranged widely, encompassing elements of architectural design, not having discipline-based departments, instruction, controlling student behavior, and staff restrooms. The board of education supported teacher choice and believed that teachers would be most effective where there was a good "fit" between them and the school. Teaching assignments were made by choice of schools, then on seniority, and finally on teaching specialization and certification. The latter was essential to ensuring that both schools had faculty to support their respective academic programs. Welch recalled, "We wanted people at East Jessamine High School who wanted to be here, and we were elated the way it turned out."

Relationships among Teachers and Administrators

Teachers don't necessarily view what goes on in school holistically. Many tend to focus narrowly on what goes on in their classrooms and relegate responsibilities, like student discipline, to school administrators. When that occurs, there is very little interplay between teachers and administration. As Young noted, "Those roles seem to be rigidly defined. When we tried to get teachers to accept broader responsibilities for student behavior, we met with some resistance." When teachers talked about what "they," the administrators, were going to do about student discipline or other decisions, Welch reminded them, "There is no 'they.' We tried to break down barriers to effective discipline by moving toward sharing that responsibility among all of us in the community. That is a defining part of not only teacher-administrator relationships but teacher-student relationships as well."

Changing the concept of schools, how things are done, and the attitudes of people who work in schools is not easy. For example, one of the most prevalent complaints about administrators at East Jessamine High School is that they are too student centered. Many teachers believe that what administrators are supposed to do is control students. They send students to the office to be disciplined, but as Welch put it, "We listen to what kids say. We maintain the respect students deserve but that doesn't mean we don't mete out punishment they deserve." To some teachers in the school, that's not the way things are supposed to happen, and occasionally they refer to East Jessamine High School as "the feel good school." Welch reacted, saying, "I take that as a huge compliment!"

Relationships among Teachers

In thinking about how teachers would relate to one another in the new school, Welch and others were realistic; they knew all faculty involved. As he said, "People are people. They have foibles, and there were times when they disagreed with one another, but for the most part we had very good relationships." Administrators in the new high school were very visible, often attending and participating in classes both as learners and as teachers. For example, Welch stopped into a class in which the teacher was explaining the Gilgamesh Epoch, and some of the students were struggling with the idea of historical time lines. After a while he asked, "Can I take a stab at that" and explained it in a different way. Then the class continued with their discussion. After school the teacher came in and said, "The children enjoyed that discussion so much and enjoyed seeing the principal come in and talk about what they were learning." All three administrators believe that being visible in the school, being in classrooms, looking at student work, and talking with students as well as teachers about what they are doing contribute to people constructing a shared view of schools and foster bonding. In this community of learners, administrators are also teachers, and their participation is not disruptive but is an integral part of the "strange attractor" that holds the community together.

As Owens Saylor, an assistant principal, recalled, "At the 'old' Jessamine County High School, we had a rather traditional notion of the structure of school. When we moved over here, things began to change. They changed because teachers recognized that we were going to work together to make decisions, that every voice is an important part of the community; and in many instances those ideas, attitudes, and ways of working influenced their relationships with students." Saylor went on to observe, "Some teachers began taking on roles that were traditionally reserved for administrators, knowing that we are all part of the same community and we all had a stake in the school. That is at the core of what we are about." During the first year, some teachers embraced these ideas more enthusiastically than others did. As Welch commented, "Teachers ran the gamut in their level of understanding of the notion of a community of learners and levels of commitment to it. To many teachers, the school's environment is still a bit threatening, and a few still don't get it."

In the past, teachers were constantly frustrated by students who were tardy to class and shifted responsibility for controlling the problem to administrators. If students were late, they were sent to the office to sit for ninety minutes. This is a complex issue. If class is interrupted, other students in class are affected. On the other hand, the student isn't accomplishing much learning by doing penance in the office. As Saylor recalled, "Faculty were very much involved in examining this issue and found that an important contributing factor to disruptive student behavior is low academic achievement. We concluded that keeping them out of class was counterproductive. It was one of the few times I can ever recall teachers quickly arriving at broad consensus. We did away with the traditional way of handling tardies and agreed that students should be in class learning." They decided to deal with students' behavior as a separate issue from instruction and handled it after school. This decision was a good example of how those in the school shifted their thinking away from control to what was important in the school: learning. As Young noted, "By the end of the year, many teachers said that they appreciated that our actions matched our rhetoric about participatory decision making." Developing a shared responsibility for decision making, however, continues to be a slow journey.

Relationships among Students and Administrators

An important part of forging good relationships with students is gaining a better understanding of them as they go about their daily work. One of the most important decisions on which administrators came to consensus was to also teach in the school. As Welch explained, "Our past experience validates the fact that teachers can make a difference in the lives of students. Administrators gain several advantages by being in the classroom. First, we can say to students and teachers that we are all members of this community and that for us the most important thing happening in the school is what's happening in the classroom, not in the office." At East Jessamine High School, the office didn't take priority over learning. Instruction was not interrupted by routine calls for students to go to the office or announcements. All three administrators viewed themselves primarily as teachers. Administrators concurred that viewing themselves and being viewed by others primarily as teachers had a positive effect on how they handled student discipline problems. They believed that when they established relationships with students as learners, it completely changed the dynamics of the principal-student discussion. As Saylor remarked, "Even in cases where we didn't have students in class, they knew that what we value is learning, not control."

For the most part, the 860 students at East Jessamine High School were unaccustomed to being asked their opinions. At the beginning of the 1997–1998 school year, the school surveyed entering students as part of an effort to develop a handbook of student rights and responsibilities. It was part of a process intended to change the language that attends discipline and how it is viewed. Students displayed a deep and enduring anger describing how they have been treated, using explicit and rather unflattering terms. A survey completed by the Prichard Committee's Partnership for Kentucky Schools, *Students Speak: How Kentucky Middle and High School Students View Schools*, released in 1997, also focused on how students view their treatment in schools. The report found that students overwhelmingly perceived that schools were primarily concerned with control, order, and discipline.

Administrators at East Jessamine High School opened a dialogue among students, teachers, and administrators, and over the course of a year, there was a perceptible shift in attitudes of both students and staff regarding the notion of discipline. During these conversations, Welch cautioned teachers about the need to avoid, "making the minor, major." He always ended the morning announcements with the comment "Have a great day, and learn a lot." In May 1998, at the conclusion of the first year, administrators surveyed students again asking them how they felt about their treatment in school and what they thought of teachers and administrators. "One of the most gratifying things of the entire year was to read their responses," Welch revealed. "The phrase I kept muttering under my breath was 'They got it. They got it.' Ninety percent of them were writing things like 'Learning is most important' and 'You think everybody ought to do their best.' I'm sure for some of them these comments were just platitudes, but it was apparent from what many of them wrote, they actually understood what we were talking about!" Even if students were echoing clichés, they were saying things about their school that were remarkably different from what they said when they entered and what their counterparts were saying in schools throughout Kentucky. Welch ended his commencement speech with the phrase "Have a great life," and the students in response said, "Learn a lot!" He said, "At that moment, I knew they got the message that learning is fantastic."

Changing Roles: Students as Learners and Teachers

Before the school opened, Welch and the principal of the "old" high school gave seniors the same opportunities to learn, compare, and talk about both schools as was given teachers. The notion of a community of learners, how it would function, and its emphasis on the responsibility of students for their own learning intrigued many. Although attendance boundaries for each school were drawn up by the board of education, seniors persuasively argued that, like teachers, they also should be given the opportunity to choose which high school they wanted to attend. The superintendent, Larry Allen, agreed and asked the board of education to allow them to make that choice. District administrators and principals thought, in all probability, most seniors would want to remain at the old high school where they had friends and familiar surroundings. The outcome of their choice was startling: two-thirds of all seniors in the district elected to attend the new high school! Welch cautioned, "Some of them came because they thought it was going to be a chaotic place and they would be able to get away with a lot more than they would at the old school. But many of them came because they got a glimpse of the ideas in which we strongly believed."

An important catalyst in the glue that holds a community of learners together involves changing the role of students, viewing them as both learners and teachers. It is evident that the school eagerly searches for creative ways to transform mundane and routine activities into extraordinary occasions for students to assume greater responsibility for learning and leadership. Welch asked students to take responsibility for surveying students' preferences for soft drinks and analyze proposals submitted by competing vendors. He said, "This activity provides opportunities for students to learn about marketing, statistics, and contractor relations. Contractors, however, were not used to our giving this level of responsibility to students." In traditional school settings, students are often relegated to positions of being passive recipients of knowledge. In a community of learners, however, students are actively engaged as knowledge providers. They individually and collaboratively generate, share, and act on information.

During the first year East Jessamine High School was in operation, relations between students and teachers began changing. Some teachers, particularly those in music and technology, viewed highly competent students as both learners and teachers. In the music program, for example, many students were virtuoso performers who assisted teachers by helping other students learn advanced techniques. This led to remarkable progress among students in the program. Improving technology and expanding its use in teaching and learning is an important, districtwide priority. Several obstacles, however, impeded progress. First, technical assistance contracts were costly, and not being able to get teachers the help they needed, when they needed it, often frustrated their efforts to integrate technology with classroom instruction.

The district coordinator for technology and extended school services, Dr. Carol Utay, worked with teachers and students to establish an innovative Student Technology Leadership Program (STLP). It identified highly competent students who were paid by the district to deliver technical assistance services to students and teachers. This initiative not only proved cost-effective and improved service delivery but also changed how many students were viewed by teachers.

The Capstone Program provided opportunities for highly capable students to extend their knowledge by completing a senior project. Owens Saylor, the program adviser, said, "Many students were surprised when I asked them how we were going to grade the projects. Students were not used to being asked to give input into how the class was going to be structured, defining parameters for projects, or evaluating them. We took time to talk about these issues, and, in my opinion, the plans we came up with were much better than I could have done alone."

Although there are many other instances of how the nature of learning and teaching changed, not all were successful. The individuals involved viewed these situations as opportunities to learn from failure. They analyzed what went wrong and how it could be improved. Reflecting back on when the school first opened, Young recalled, "Students would say things like, 'It didn't work because we felt the teachers were . . . ,' and we would respond saying, 'You misunderstand—you are responsible for this!' That was an important part of their learning." By the end of the year, students were taking responsibility for implementing their ideas, including giving seniors complete responsibility for planning their prom and graduation ceremonies.

SUPERINTENDENT SUPPORT FOR INNOVATION

The superintendent, Larry Allen, wanted to create an unconventional high school, one that embraced the principles expressed in KERA. His interest opened an extraordinary potential for student learning, captured the enthusiasm and commitment of those working in the district, and gave voice to a wide array of people in making education decisions. His passion for learning provided a template for making child-centered decisions. Kentucky's education reform milieu, launched by KERA in 1990, challenged educators to improve instruction. A few, like teachers and administrators in Jessamine County, found it highly complementary to their new-generational views on how schooling may be fundamentally changed.

Although the superintendent was regarded as a visionary, a risk taker, and an advocate for children who accomplished a great deal, he acknowledges that his work was made easier by an extraordinary set of circumstances that unfolded in the district over the prior decade. He was able to institutionalize the notion of a community of learners, a radically different concept of schooling, because his work was grounded in a decade graced both by continuity in district leadership and consistency in board of education policy. Although the relationship between successive district superintendents and changing membership on the board of education may have created problems for both, their common desire to improve schooling and create opportunities for children to learn provided a powerful bond and a basis for transcending political differences. Teachers, administrators, parents, and citizens of Jessamine County were pleased but not surprised to learn that Allen was selected as the Kentucky Association of School Administrators Superintendent of the Year and was its representative to the American Association of School Administrators (AASA) Superintendent of the Year competition in 1998. Allen retired in 1997 and now serves in a variety of consultative roles.

Linda France was an outstanding teacher in Jessamine County who was nurtured in the district's long-standing progressive education environment. France had been a teacher when Don Martin was superintendent and was one of those empowered and supported by him as well as superintendents who followed. She has a strong dedication to children, clear vision of the importance of improving student learning, and is a powerful advocate for empowering teachers and administrators to make decisions about teaching and learning. These qualities helped her become a middle school assistant principal and later, assistant superintendent for curriculum and instruction during Allen's administration. She worked closely with Tom Welch during the formative years when the new East Jessamine High School was being fashioned as a community of learners. When Allen announced his retirement in the spring of 1998, France was approached by colleagues in the district who helped convince her to apply for the position. She applied and was selected by the board of education to be the new superintendent of Jessamine County. She assumed her duties in the 6,400-student district in July 1998 and, like her predecessors, is uncommonly supportive of child-centered innovations and the notion of a community of learners.

CONSISTENCY AMID REFORM: A LONGITUDINAL PERSPECTIVE

In retrospect, continuity in the superintendency and consistency in board of education policy from 1983 to 1999 appeared to be golden threads in the warp and weft of Jessamine County's education reform initiative. Shared beliefs in the primacy of children and their learning served as guiding principles, provided a template for planning, and furnished a litmus test for decisions. Continuity in leadership and consistency in board of education policy making over the long term created the circumstances for substantive change to take root and flourish.

5

Faced with a Hostile Press

C. Cryss Brunner

PRIMARY FOCUS OF THE CASE

The purpose of this case study is to examine how an urban superintendent responded to a "crisis in representation" (Ellsworth, 1994), with the intent that such an examination will be instructive for other superintendents faced with similar challenges. This crisis was created when a newspaper dominated a community and its school district by using what many participants reported to be "purposeful misrepresentation." And while this particular case occurred in an urban setting, the event is instructive for educators in communities of all types and sizes.

KEY LEARNING OBJECTIVES

- To examine the nature and effects of power relationships
- To discover possible implications of media hostility
- To understand the political ramifications of media representation
- To design a possible action plan
- To explore the public relations responsibilities of the superintendency
- To reflect on the responsibilities of the superintendent to the community
- To establish a sense of the personal costs for superintendents who face these challenges
- To examine the legal aspects of the case (as they relate to state and local laws)
- To explore the impact of media on boards of education and, consequently, on the relationship between boards of education and superintendents

BACKGROUND: THE MEDIA

At one time or another, our sprawling educational enterprise with its 105,000 schools, 46 million students, 2.2 million teachers, and 15,500 school districts engages the energies of nearly one-third of our population. And the success or failure of this massive endeavor, as we are reminded hourly, will have a crucial impact on the American future. How could any journalist resist an opportunity to chronicle and interpret this vast story (Kaplan, 1992, p. 23)?

Clearly, journalists do not resist this opportunity. Almost daily, even in the smallest of communities, a story related to education finds its way into the media. To be sure, some reporting seems balanced—telling the good and the bad news about education. But consider the assertion from veteran publicist Frank Mankiewicz that "sooner or later everybody will know the dirty little secret of American journalism, that the reports are wrong. . . . Whenever you see a news story you were part of, it is always wrong" (quoted in Kaplan, 1992, p. 15).

Common sense alone tells us that it is difficult to include everything that belongs in a story, that it is impossible to know exactly what should be considered news in the first place. Even Herbert Gans's scholarly work *Deciding What's News* (1980) has only partially succeeded in balancing the forces that make such decisions (Kaplan, 1992). In short, there is an awareness on the part of journalists that even the "best" reporting is "wrong." Journalists admit that even in the best of situations, few people receive what their partisans consider to be accurate and balanced coverage (Kaplan, 1992).

Beyond this awareness, there is concern even among people who are editors, journalists, media analysts, and communication/media experts regarding what is considered by many to be a decline in the credibility of journalism.

Important questions to consider: What if a press decides to purposely report only negative news, to purposely slant the news in a way that is damaging? What about the ethics of reporting? In a capitalist society, does the question of what sells take precedence over ethics? And what does damaging reporting about public schools mean for the students and educators?

CENTRAL CHARACTERS

The primary participant, Dr. Kelly, was a forty-seven-year-old, European American superintendent who was in the first year of her third superintendency at the time of the study. She had a doctorate in educational administration and had nine years of superintendency experience at the time of the study. Dr. Kelly was considered by a panel of experts (and by those who had worked with her in other districts and settings) to be one of the most exceptional superintendents in the nation.

The primary media in this case was a newspaper. (*Newspaper* is used throughout the chapter in place of the actual name of the paper studied.) Although just one of three newspapers in the county, the *Newspaper* was considered by participants as the most influential, the most powerful—in fact the *Newspaper* was the singularly most influential media vehicle in most of the county.

THE SETTING

This case took place in a large urban school district (over 130,000 students) in the Southeast (an urban area of about 1.3 million people). Data were collected from records, documents, participant and nonparticipant observation, and over seventy-two in-depth interviews that were recorded and transcribed. Interviews were conducted with school district personnel (teachers, administrators, staff), community members (political figures, business people, parents, students), board of education members, journalists, and the superintendent. At least twelve of the seventy-two interviews were conducted with the superintendent over a period of four years.

Laws that impacted the case were what the state called the "Sunshine Laws." Under these laws, any documents, E-mails, mail to the superintendent or other employees of the district, and anything else in writing were considered public property and thus available to the press. All meetings were open to the press with the exception of meetings for the purpose of personnel actions. In this extreme situation, the press had the audacity—and the right—to open the superintendent's mail before she got it. Furthermore, the press had access to all of the superintendent's evaluation documents.

THE STORY

The Press and Its Use of Power

One businessman interviewed described the *Newspaper* in this way:

> One of the reasons the *Newspaper* is such an anomaly is because it is a privately held company. Privately held companies behave differently than publicly held companies. So that dynamic is different. . . . But at another level, the one thing I find objectionable about the *Newspaper* is that the *Newspaper* comes in and is surprisingly personal in both its news reporting and particularly in its editorial position. So, that's a really important thing. . . . I think they're *not* [original emphasis] constructive. . . . The *Newspaper* has a vindictive kind of a feel to it. And clearly, the *Newspaper* is the singularly most influential media vehicle in most of this county.

It was evident, from the interviews (even early in the study), that the *Newspaper* was perceived to define and use power as "power over" people and things (Clegg, 1989; Hartsock, 1981). Consider the statement made by a school district administrator: "The *Newspaper* sees itself as being a social engineer, and that's fine. But they are not objective, and they choose sides. And being a social engineer, they also want to be the boss."

A press that wants to be boss may not sound that unusual to the reader. But, as I continued to listen to those I interviewed, the issue of the negative reporting by the *Newspaper* was on people's minds. Many were angry about what they considered unfair and abusive use of power by the press. Unsolicited remarks were made in myriad interviews. For example, people who had a wide variety of experiences with the media, in other communities, made powerful statements about the viciousness of what people considered the "attack mode" of the *Newspaper*. One board of education member said:

> What do you do when a newspaper's got an editorial staff, if not a news staff, that's in attack mode—confrontational—that's just any kind of nasty attitude that you can imagine about the way they approach problems and issues?
>
> I've *never* [original emphasis] seen a newspaper that attacks individuals in their editorials. They may attack an issue or an approach, but rarely, if ever, will they say something negative about an individual whom they name or a group of individuals whom they name. And the *Newspaper* does that as common practice. I mean, it's just—it's rude. They had an editorial about my predecessor on the board. They said, "She's not fit to run a lemonade stand." That doesn't belong in a quality newspaper editorial. And it's crazy. . . for a while there it was fascinating—I would call them up, you know, and compliment them on a particular stance that they took, or I would take issue with them on something. I'm pretty blatantly open, as you can probably tell. I'm trusting, I guess. I don't think of people as being diabolical—like I don't think that they will look for things in what I say to use against me. And yet, when I talked to the editorial people from the [*Newspaper*], for a time there, I could almost count on three or four or five days later that my name would come up in an editorial about something that was totally different than what the focus of the conversation was. They would pick something out of the conversation that I had with them, on some other issue, and chastise me for my point of view. Fascinating, you know. We weren't even engaging in that conversation. But they used something I said out of context in a way to talk about me negatively.

A media analyst who was a former journalist confirmed the board member's sense that his words were used out of context.

> With the [*Newspaper*], what you find is that you may be talking about apples, and then during the conversation there are two or three sentences about oranges, and then two or three days later, that little piece of orange information comes out in a really negative way. So, they're deciphering only their own agenda's information and cutting that out of the conversations—cutting out the pieces that will support their own agenda. So it becomes extremely frustrating to even have a dialogue with them.

A board member made this comment:

> And the people here are so used to it that they think all newspapers do this—they think it is common practice. And all this negativity when so much good stuff, exciting stuff

is happening. What's such a shame is that if the *Newspaper* would refocus their energies in a positive direction, the whole county could just pop all at once in terms of the positive things that could happen. Even if the reporting was just balanced. It could be remarkable what would happen in short order here.

Almost everyone I interviewed agreed with this man's statement that "people were so used to" the abusive behavior from the *Newspaper*. Even with two other newspapers in the county that were much more balanced in their reporting, the community was "silenced" by "attacks" from the *Newspaper*.

Other participants in the study talked about the damage that the *Newspaper*'s dominating negative press was doing to the community and to the schools. One parent reflected, "The school system always looks worse [in the paper] than it really is." One school district administrator described the situation this way:

> You would think that the business people would be concerned about the negative press [about the school system]. But everybody is waiting for someone else to do something. It's a vicious circle. I don't care about who they're talking about in the paper or what the paper slams next; it still affects the perception of the entire system. The other piece is, I think it's going to be very difficult to recruit people to a district where there is such great potential for people to be constantly torn apart. So why would they want to come?
>
> In fact, we've had a couple of students speak up about the fact that they were tired of being portrayed [by the press] as the kids in trouble all of the time. They said, "Yes, some of us are in trouble sometimes, but that is not all of the story."

A high school teacher confirmed the comments quoted here when he expressed his concerns:

> You know, the students never hear anything good about what they do. And people really want to hear it. They would feed on it, you know. I mean people like to get a pat on the back. The only ones [students] that get the recognition are the ones who bring a gun to school. Or the ones who bring a knife to school. And when I was being interviewed [he was Teacher of the Year], I said it's the media's fault. And I said that. I said they don't spend enough time focusing on the positives. And how we are going to change that? I have no idea.

All of the data, including my analysis of articles in the community's three papers, led me to believe that the *Newspaper* was purposely misrepresenting the school district. Perhaps the most powerful of all, however, was an interview with a journalist who worked for the *Newspaper*. He stated that "the [*Newspaper*] had a very dysfunctional approach to coverage of school district news" and that there was an "undue focus on what doesn't work." He believed that the editorial approach to the school district and to the superintendent had "seeped into the newsroom"—something that is not supposed to happen. He explained that the editorial board might pass judgment and draw conclusions, but the newsroom is supposed to be objective, balanced, factual, and not supposed to draw conclusions.

I determined through interviews and documents that not only had the editorial board at the *Newspaper* represented the district in a narrowly negative way, but also its perceptions had become the dominant "official knowledge" about the district. The district was silenced as a result, unable to represent itself. Clearly, the *Newspaper* used power as domination over others or as "power over." In fact, individuals reported that the editorial board used vindictiveness at a personal level as a way to control people. These actions on the part of the press created a "crisis in representation" for the school district.

The Press's View of the Superintendent

Dr. Kelly's beginning in the district was, to say the least, rocky. In fact, before she even took the job, the *Newspaper* was filled with articles that even the most conservative reader would consider scathing. When Dr. Kelly was offered the job, her first step was the negotiation of a contract. It should be noted that the district wanted Dr. Kelly to start the job in March before she had finished her job in her previous district. The district was struggling along with an interim superintendent while they did the search. So, Dr. Kelly literally worked between districts from the time of her hiring in January until March 15 when she officially took the position doing the job of superintendent in both districts. Her contract negotiations necessarily reflected this unusual demand on her time and strength and were not considered unusual or out of line by anyone who was familiar with such negotiations.

The typically uneventful process of contract negotiations became the target of a full-blown media attack. The media frenzy lasted for almost twenty days. And although I do not have all of the articles related to this topic in my stack of data, I have forty-six articles and editorials from the two primary newspapers in the district. Out of these articles and editorials, thirty-five are from the *Newspaper*.

After an initial article, "[Kelly] Ups Ante: $–.– Plus Perks" (January 24, 1996, p. 1B), which proclaimed that Dr. Kelly's "proposal doesn't resemble the school district's offer," the next article led with the headline "Callers Blast Kelly's 'Ridiculous' Requests" (January 25, 1996, p. 1A). The article quoted callers who said things such as "Never heard of anything so ridiculous in all my life," "She should take a walk," and "Tell her we're sorry and bring in the other candidates." The article also reflected Dr. Kelly's surprise that the early stages of the negotiations were made so public, and while the *Newspaper* used her surprise to make her look ignorant, Dr. Kelly at the time was a superintendent in a district in the same state and very experienced with the laws governing public records.

An article from the other primary paper in the district told a different story:

> Board Chairwoman [Name] and Vice-Chairman [Name] issued a joint statement saying the board anticipated the current offer-and-counteroffer process and said they were disappointed it had become an "incendiary media event."
>
> "[Dr. Kelly], the [state's] Superintendent of the Year, possesses excellent educational leadership and business management skills needed by this school district at this time,"

the statement said. "We look forward to working together . . . to accomplish the district's mission."

Dr. Kelly's requests caused an uproar among people who saw her demands as outrageous and said the board should not hire her. "A lot of people don't understand the negotiation process," board member [Name] said (*Second Paper,* January 27, 1996, p. 1B).

Two days later, the *Newspaper* published an editorial titled "Think of Schools First, Not of [Kelly's] Wish List" (January 30, 1996, editorial page). One sentence in enlarged text stated, "Her attitude jeopardizes voter approval of a badly-needed special tax for construction." In this particular editorial, the *Newspaper's* allegiance to the superintendent, Dr. Sanderson (pseudonym)—who preceded Dr. Kelly—can be detected:

> [School District] School Board members have made a worse mess of trying to hire a new superintendent than they did of firing the last one. . . .
>
> Now board members who would not even evaluate, much less support, [Dr. Sanderson] are expressing unquestioned confidence in someone whom they haven't even hired. They are scheduled to meet Wednesday night to discuss negotiations with Dr. [Kelly]. When they do, they should consider how harmful Dr. [Kelly's] attitude—and theirs—will be to chances of voters passing a special tax for new schools and an important law designed to eliminate crowded schools.
>
> Dr. [Kelly] can't be blamed for requesting that she get a four-year contract with automatic renewals, given the board's costly decision to fire [Dr. Sanderson] without cause. [In fact, cause was public.] But Dr. [Kelly's] request for *guaranteed* annual 5 percent raises ([Dr. Sanderson] got no raises) insults all teachers, bus drivers and other employees who haven't had a decent raise in years and won't for some time. Her demands for a car (model specified) and closing costs on her current home insult taxpayers.
>
> Dr. [Kelly's] supporters picked her because they said she knows how to bring a community together. Instead, she has angered the community before even taking the job. (*Newspaper,* January 30, 1996, editorial page)

In this editorial, the *Newspaper* links Dr. Kelly's request for more money—than the board of education initially offered her—with overcrowded schools. In this linking, the impression was left with readers that Dr. Kelly's salary would prevent the school district from addressing the bad conditions that existed for the students. On the other hand, the second primary press in the district quoted a couple of people whom they believed help explain the media frenzy. For example, in an article dated January 30, 1996, education writers wrote:

> [Kelly's] contract requests may have done more damage than normal because she is coming into a district that already has two black eyes, [Name] said.
>
> "That is a huge problem that this is a small symptom of—the reservoir of anger that is already there, that was there for [former superintendent—two superintendents before

Kelly] and that was exacerbated by [Dr. Sanderson]," [Name] said. "If the level of satisfaction were higher, this wouldn't have drawn as much attention." (p. 1B)

Thus, while the second primary press was a part of the media attack especially in
editorials, it gave significant space to explanations for the extreme nature of the
onslaught. Furthermore, the second press was not protecting Dr. Sanderson but rather
reflecting an opinion that I came to understand was more in keeping with the
district's and the community's.

This was just the beginning of the story. And while it would be false to claim that
every article was negative, the *Newspaper*'s attacks did not stop after Dr. Kelly's contract was signed. For example, when she asked her area and assistant superintendents
to read Lee Bolman and Terrance Deal's book *Leading with Soul* (1996), one *Newspaper* article—titled "[Kelly's] Suggested Reading: It's Gibran Gone Corporate" (February 16, 1996, p. 1D)—focused sarcastically on her request and stated "[*Leading
with Soul*] offers a watery theology of common decency most suitable for minds that
can't quite grasp the deep moral concepts embodied in the Star Wars philosophy of
the Force."

One noticeable and frequently used strategy employed by the *Newspaper* was to
commend the two board of education members who commonly took positions
against Dr. Kelly—who in fact were the two who did not vote to hire her—and to
make any board member who agreed with her or supported her look foolish. This
type of publicity over time for board members drives a wedge between the superintendent and the board and creates public opinion that board members who are supportive of the superintendent need to be replaced in the next election.

WHY THE ATTACK? EDUCATORS' AND OTHER COMMUNITY
MEMBERS' ANSWER

When I asked people why they thought Dr. Kelly was the target of the *Newspaper*'s
attacks, many participants pointed out that Dr. Kelly was not the *Newspaper*'s first
choice during the superintendent selection process. A media analyst reported that
in her previous position, a district of sixty thousand students, Dr. Kelly had a very
good relationship with the media—not cozy, but certainly not strictly confrontational. I asked him for his opinion regarding the reason that the *Newspaper* was so
hostile.

Well, (a) she was not the "chosen one" for the [*Newspaper*], and (b) the [*Newspaper*] is
vindictive in its approach, and (c) the school district was in terrible shape when she
came in, and it was hostile at the time because of previous events. And Dr. [Kelly's]
approach has been not about protecting herself or her image, but one of working to
do what can be done to build a good school system. And, you simply cannot have a
good educational system without public support. And the [*Newspaper*] seems to have
a campaign to deride and discredit Dr. [Kelly]. And you asked me "Why?" and when

you do that, you're asking me to get into their heads, and that's tough. I can only speculate. I mean, it could just be ego; it could be to stir up reader interest; it could be human frailties of feeling defeated so you come out swinging. Who knows? Who knows? Some people in the newspaper business, or just in the media business, thrive on controversy, that's all. And then, of course, that sells more papers too. So if they write nice things that aren't controversial, they don't thrive.

An influential member of the business community confirmed the media analyst's comments:

> It's the most negative stuff I've ever dealt with in the newspapers—they're mean. And in terms of the schools, there must be fifty editorials a year about the schools. And very personal, too. In fact, the superintendent—she was quoted in ninety some editorials in a year. So, about a third of the editorials have been about the superintendent of the schools.

A journalist in the community echoed the information quoted here and was another who indicated that Dr. Kelly was not the *Newspaper's* choice for superintendent. He stated that the superintendent who preceded Dr. Kelly had the complete support of the *Newspaper's* editorial board—they were editorially committed to Dr. Sanderson (pseudonym for the former superintendent). Even when Dr. Sanderson was forced out of her position because of a multitude of errors and bad judgment (which were documented and publicly known and were, in part, the reason for hostility in the school district), the *Newspaper* stood by her. He added that newspapers typically hold to the notion that they should never admit they are wrong and certainly should never change their position once taking a stand. Thus, when Dr. Kelly was hired, and she was not their candidate of choice, the *Newspaper* immediately cast her as someone wearing a "black hat."

THE SUPERINTENDENT AND HER USE OF POWER

When I asked Dr. Kelly to define power, she said, "Power is the ability to get things done through other people." She continued:

> If we worry less about who gets credit and more about getting it done, it's remarkable what you can get done. . . . I'm much more comfortable saying "we" did it, because, first of all, that's the truth. I mean single-handedly, I don't know what I get done other than walk in the door. I think that everything else that happens is through the strength of the people that surround me. I don't want to be an expert in everything. And the only way that the power would be mine is if I had all the information and all the knowledge. And I just don't think that's the way it happens.
> Q. What happens when that belief system disappears?
> A. I think a good example might be in what I hear happened in the district that

I've left. People say that now the decisions are more or less made by one or two people—that others are not either involved in or do they see themselves as responsible for the implementation. I think that is what happens as soon as you isolate decision making to a few people. That's why even in our cabinet meetings there are people who come and go. What I mean by that is that they might not be there all of the time, but if we're working on certain issues, I involve those people because they need to give their input, but also because they need to see the attitude of the senior staff. I think that if you didn't do that, you wouldn't necessarily get the same outcome. I just don't think you get the same things done.

Clearly, Dr. Kelly's concept of power requires that she work "with/to" others. She believes strongly in input for decision making—she expects it from everyone, and here's how she conveys her expectations to others:

Q. How do people come to understand that you expect them to give input and to get input from others?
A. I continually ask questions, like "Well?" and "Who said that?" And they answer, "That was so and so." And I say, "Well, let's get them here." I want them to understand that their responsibility is to bring all the people to the table. And it's probably one of the hardest things for them to catch on to. They get better, and then there's like little relapses. And the relapses occur when we are working on the most intense issues. I mean, the more intense the issue is, the less likelihood they will demonstrate the inclusion piece. The more intense, the more they feel like they have to control the input.

To triangulate Dr. Kelly's perceptions and self-reports, I asked everyone I interviewed to answer three questions: In your opinion, how might Dr. Kelly define power? How does Dr. Kelly make decisions? How does Dr. Kelly get things done? The following narratives are representative examples of their responses.

A board member made observations about the way she worked with the board:

She has a team approach. I mean, we heard from her lips that the team of eight people, the seven board members and the superintendent, needed to do some things. And we bought into not only the letter of it, but the spirit of it. . . . I have an attitude that if I'm really comfortable and I'm not insecure, I don't have any problem with sharing decision making. And in my opinion, of some other board members, either in this district or in other counties, is that those people feel insecure for whatever reasons, and that they have great difficulty sharing what they perceive to be their power.

A high school teacher also talked about Dr. Kelly's ability to work with others:

I think she was very smart in really getting input from a lot of different areas in the school district when she came in. . . . She knows that a lot of the power in the school district depends on the power in the business community and other organizations in the county, and she tried to tie them together. I think she does at least listen to what they say. . . . I think she's very collaborative.

One political figure in the community talked about the way Dr. Kelly made things happen:

> I think she would say that it is the ability to make things happen in a positive way. . . . and that way would be through collaboration. I see some real, what I consider democratic, action occurring in this district, and I think now we have a superintendent that is very capable to work with that and embellish that and embrace that and support that.

An administrator talked about her work with the administrative staff:

> Dr. Kelly is big on team work, big on collaboration. . . . Dr. Kelly listens. . . . She is very much willing to allow the meeting to collaborate to the point where I personally am falling off the chair. Because that's not my style. I mean I run a meeting and sometimes get criticized for not letting everybody get their say.
> Q. Is there value in being collaborative?
> A. If your idea of collaboration is truly to bring people to the table and to try to come to consensus or to a decision, then I think it is very important because I am of the opinion that you have to have people who are involved, who are affected by a decision, involved in that decision.

While the strongest evidence of Dr. Kelly's definition and use of power came in interviews, there was also evidence in many of the local presses, including the *Newspaper*. Consider the following quotes from the two primary papers:

> [Kelly] says she won't be successful unless district officials, residents, and community and business leaders work together on several key issues facing her administration. . . .
> [Kelly] says she isn't planning a major administrative shakeup, and her new staff is included in nearly all decision-making. (*Newspaper,* March 17, 1996, p. 2B)

A headline in the second primary press of the community read "[Kelly] Wants Public to Get More Involved." The article contained the following statement: "Several [Name] Elementary teachers in attendance were pleased with [Kelly's] remarks when it came to ethics and community involvement" (*Second Paper,* March 22, 1996, p. 1B).

During the course of the interviews and from the newspapers, I learned that a shared power profile had many components. To describe them all is beyond the scope of this chapter, but after hearing the interviews and reading the papers, it was clear that Dr. Kelly defined and used power in collaborative, consensus-building, coactive, or interactive ways (Follett, 1942; Sarason, 1990).

EXERCISES FOR STUDENTS

1. Step into the superintendent's shoes and design an action plan that you believe will address the situation.

2. Clearly, Dr. Kelly defined and used power in a collaborative way. Describe a response to this situation that would be "walking the talk" of this use of power. How would a superintendent who defined and used power as dominance and control respond?

3. How would you feel in a similar situation? Could you handle it? Why? Why not?

4. What do you think happened next? Write your version of "The Rest of the Story."

5. Does your state have laws like the "Sunshine Laws" in this case? What laws affect media coverage in your district?

6. How would board of education members in your district act under this type of press attack?

7. What are the implications for a school district when the local media is negative? What are the implications for a community's economic health when the media is negative about local schools? What are the implications for public schools when media at the national level is negative? What are the possible ramifications for students when the media is negative about public schools?

THE REST OF THE STORY

The Superintendent's View of and Approach to the Press

I didn't ask Dr. Kelly direct questions about her view of the *Newspaper;* rather, I (1) paid close attention during interviews to anything she said in passing, (2) observed how she acted in response to different things the *Newspaper* did, (3) listened to what others said Dr. Kelly had done or said about the press, and (4) interviewed a district administrator who had the responsibility of working directly with the staff at the *Newspaper.* In this section, I share narrative and observation data that falls into those four categories.

Narrative Data

During one interview with Dr. Kelly, I asked her to compare her past experiences with those she was having at the time of the interview. She talked a bit about the differences she saw between press experiences of the past and present: "The [*Newspaper*] will print things—I mean, the more controversial the better. They seem to work to present it in a way that doesn't make the school district look good. And that is a very different approach from my previous experience with the press."

In another conversation, I asked her how things were going, what she was learning. She responded, "Well, one of the things I am kept in touch with constantly is humility." I continued, "How does that happen?" She answered quickly, "The press teaches me."

Observations and Records

In a televised board of education meeting, Dr. Kelly publicly thanked the press for bringing issues to her attention that needed to be addressed. She added that the press, in essence, served the district when they used their time and staff to pursue these issues. These comments were made after a story was reported by the *Newspaper* in a very damaging manner. The problem that was the focus of the story was something that needed to be "fixed," but the reporting was a personal attack on Dr. Kelly, when in fact the problem preexisted her tenure.

In an administrative council meeting, one of Dr. Kelly's central office administrators asked her how she would respond to the press's aggressiveness. She replied that her response could not be "in kind." Basically, she believed that she should practice the adage "Treat others as you want to be treated."

The Views of Educators and Other Community Members

One teacher in the district recalled something Dr. Kelly had said that was representative of reports from others interviewed: "During the first meeting she had at our school, she said that she couldn't make or break herself or make decisions solely based on what the media thought because many times the media doesn't represent the public. And the more I become involved in public education, the more critical I am of the media."

Interview with District Administrator

In an interview with a district administrator who worked directly with the *Newspaper*, I came to more fully understand Dr. Kelly's approach to the press. First, he stated that Dr. Kelly had told him that "you can't ignore them [the *Newspaper* and media in general], but you can't expect them to carry our water for us." He said that she continued to focus on what was the right thing to do in any situation and that she espoused the view that "we have to do what is right to get good press."

Perhaps one of the most interesting views he reported was that she believed that "public relations solutions don't work." He continued by saying she believed that public relations solutions most often were just ways to sugarcoat the truth, and she wanted no part of them. He said her policy was "No public relations," just fundamental issues related to core values—ethics, competence, and accountability. And, as an organization the school district must not only identify problems but also identify solutions.

Finally, he observed that she held to a course driven by a consistent message— "do the right thing"—and always worked to be more inclusive in terms of how information should be shared. He added that the demands of the *Newspaper* were incredible.

For example, one of the *Newspaper's* practices was to open the superintendent's mail—in the district office—before she had a chance to read it herself. This practice was in place before she came into the district, and although she was uncomfortable with it, she decided that to change it would heighten the accusations of the *Newspaper* that she was hiding something from it.

He further explained that his office/staff was being completely reorganized to meet the demands of the press. Dr. Kelly believed, he said, that the school district must meet their demands. To do otherwise would fuel animosity, because at a practical level the journalists needed information to do their work. Their animosity created "armed camps," he said, with the reporters "shaking the Sunshine Laws in the faces of school district staff."

One Year Later: Follow-up

One year after my first extended site visit, I returned to the district to do a few more in-depth interviews and gather newspaper articles to determine what effect Dr. Kelly's power with/to philosophy had on the power over practice of the *Newspaper*. What I learned in interviews was that the animosity had eased. The district administrator in charge of communications with the press told me how this had come to pass.

First, he talked about how Dr. Kelly constantly went out to the community—to organizations such as Rotary and Kiwanis—groups as small as twenty-five people. He had advised her that doing this type of thing was almost impossible because of the size of the county, but she had not followed his advice. He told me, "She deeply believes in the role of these types of service groups in society and is committed to reaching them." I also observed Dr. Kelly's commitment to being at myriad types of gatherings to communicate directly with all types of people about the importance of education.

Second, he said that the reorganization of his office enabled the school district to be more forthcoming with communication. Third, everyone was attending to the media to ensure access to information in an open and candid way. The new established attitude was "We don't want to hide it; we want to fix it." This attitude, he believed, gave the school district more credibility. "We are not at war like we once were," he stated.

Fourth, he told me that he (as a representative of the district's new position with the media) had approached the press with the questions: "How can we get you what you need?" and "How can you help us get you what you need?" He said the last question was extremely important, and once the press was somewhat convinced that the school district was delivering what they promised, the press was willing to be more reasonable in their requests for information. He shared that earlier their requests took a tremendous amount of time and manpower when, in fact, the press didn't actually need all of the information. He felt strongly that direct contacts with the editors and the reporters had helped the situation.

Fifth, he stated that the political climate was changing because of acts on the part of the state legislature. In this case, the *Newspaper* had been supporting a referendum for a one-cent sales tax that would ultimately build more schools. The act of the legislation changed how school capacity was calculated resulting in the disappearance of overcrowding (on paper) in the schools. At this point, the *Newspaper* took up the criticism of the legislature. At the same time, the district communications administrator went to the press with a message from the school district. "Our message to them was," he told me, "every time you make the school look bad, you undermine your support of the referendum." During such a situation, while the focus of the *Newspaper* had shifted to the greater evils of the legislature, he saw the *Newspaper* beginning to change the way it did business related to the news about the school district and the superintendent. At such moments, he confided, he could count on the "intellectual dishonesty" of the press. It was this type of dishonesty that he believed could help the press move to a position where Dr. Kelly would be allowed to wear a white hat instead of a black hat.

In fact, I witnessed an example of "intellectual dishonesty" during my second visit to the district. During that visit there was a lot of activity around the issue of going to the voters with a referendum for an additional half-cent sales tax to generate revenue earmarked for building more schools. In the month (December) prior to my visit, the board of education—with Dr. Kelly's recommendation—had made the decision that the referendum should go on the ballot in the fall. Board members were out in the community actively building support for yes votes.

In a surprise move, the state proclaimed that money from the lottery would be dispersed to school districts who submitted, within a short time frame, construction plans for using the funds. The funds for the district were substantial.

A flurry of meetings were held to answer questions about how much money could be used over a period of time, how much construction the district could wisely manage and properly oversee, and the wisdom of asking taxpayer for funds when, in fact, the district could use—in a practical sense—only so much money within a particular time frame. Concerns were raised about the political implications for board members, some of whom were up for reelection and who had intensely worked to gain voter support for the referendum. In addition, Dr. Kelly noted that since all of the school districts in the state were getting funds, the construction materials and labor markets would be flooded with money and contracts, resulting in skyrocketing prices.

To add more fuel to the fire, the issue of timing was critical. To allow board members to continue raising support for a referendum that may never be on the ballot not only was dangerous but also lacked integrity and was unethical. Thus, based on an ethic of "doing the right thing," in an unprecedented fashion, top-level administrators led by Dr. Kelly went to the board—who were completely unaware of the possibility—to recommend a reversal in the decision to take a referendum to the voters in the fall.

The board was stunned. Not surprisingly, they felt undermined and blindsided. The *Newspaper's* first article stated:

Schools Superintendent [Kelly] Monday recommended abandoning the campaign for a half-penny sales tax for school construction—only six weeks after pushing for it.

Among her reasons for distancing herself from the Sept. 1 vote: There might not be enough time to come up with a precise plan detailing what would be built with the money.

"It's not very doable," [Kelly] said at the school board workshop at [Name] High School.

Her argument went beyond the timetable. Despite continued crowding, she said the short-term need for dollars just isn't there, since an infusion of $___ million in lottery money will be spent over the next 18 months on an overwhelming ___ projects, big and small. And, she said, those projects will glut the construction market, driving up costs. (January 27, 1998, p. 1A)

The article continued with quotes from board members: "There is no way I can support a delay," said [board member]. "I don't expect to see incredible changes in our plan. I will not sit and allow our children to wait in the wings until we come up with the best time."

The next day, the second primary press printed the following editorial statement: "[Kelly] is only being prudent in fine-tuning her strategy to deal with a rapidly changing set of circumstances. But both board members and voters have reason to be confused by her abrupt about-face on the sales-tax vote" (*Second Paper,* editorial page).

Back to the activities of the *Newspaper:* On January 29, 1998, an editorial blasted Dr. Kelly's position. In a damning way, the editorial stated:

Her reversal reinforces the need for board members to find out whether Dr. [Kelly] shares their priorities. . . . Rather than invent excuses for delay—a *preposterous-sounding construction glut* [my emphasis], unclear state guidelines—the district should tout the schools that have been built and the need that remains.

With each delay, more students suffer. With each delay, more parents hoping for relief grow increasingly frustrated. With each delay, the chances for success grow slimmer.

Interestingly, a national newspaper, the *Wall Street Journal,* with much greater credibility than the district's own *Newspaper,* published a story on February 18, 1998, that confirmed Dr. Kelly's rationale against the fall referendum when it stated, "School districts are asking for much more classroom-construction money for the coming year than lawmakers expected, raising fears that the Legislature's new lottery-bond initiative will spark inflation in [State's] hot building market." The article continued:

Rep. [Name] and Sen. [Name], who led their chambers' efforts in crafting the program, say their big concern is the inflationary potential of injecting so much money into the market at once. Already, [State's] nonresidential construction industry is running "about as close to capacity as you can get, maybe a little over," says [Name], a University of [State] urban planning professor. "Pumping more than $1 billion into the . . . school construction sector undoubtedly would create temporary shortages," says Prof. [Name]. "Some contractors are going to find themselves in a wonderful spot," he adds. (p. F2)

How did the *Newspaper* respond to this credible source's echo of Dr. Kelly's position (which she asserted almost three weeks before the *Wall Street Journal* reported it)? On February 20, 1998, I found one article titled "School Cash Crunch II." In the middle of the article was the following paragraph:

More than two-thirds of the money has been spoken for, *The Wall Street Journal* reported this week. Lawmakers had hoped to dole it out over five years. Now they worry about school districts swamping the construction industry with orders—a concern shared by [Name] School's Superintendent Dr. [Kelly] [my emphasis]—and glutting the bond market with their bonds.

There was no mention of the *Newspaper's* editorial position that Dr. Kelly was just "making up preposterous excuses." Clearly, intellectual dishonesty was at work. In my experience, when a superintendent proposes that a tax increase be delayed, with sound business and economic reasoning, she or he is applauded loudly. Dr. Kelly's foresight in this case, however, was buried in the middle of an article and barely mentioned.

Even so, this barely mentioned piece is evidence that the *Newspaper* was slowly changing its position with Dr. Kelly. The same article moves the blame for the whole money crunch to the state legislature, something that the school district administrator in charge of communications said was happening more and more often. So, while the *Newspaper* was still on the attack, the frequency and intensity has lessened. Further, the *Newspaper* has turned its antagonistic attention away from Dr. Kelly and the school district more and more often.

I noted during my second visit that Dr. Kelly's work was making a difference in the district, a fact that gave the *Newspaper* reason to focus elsewhere. Strides were evident even amid the financial nightmare—misuse of funds, poor oversight practices, major budget cuts—that Dr. Kelly inherited from the previous administration.

Dr. Kelly held the philosophy to "tell all." She believed that mistakes as well as successes should be shared with the public. This philosophy was tough to live at times because of the multitude of poor and even illegal practices that preexisted her entering the district and, further, because of the hostile press.

The fact that the poor financial practices were not all uncovered at once but slowly, as oversight and auditing groups were put in place, added to the difficulty. Stories of overspending and misappropriation of funds continued to hit the press. Even so, the position of the district was stronger at the time of my second visit. Evidence of that newfound strength could be found in quotes from board members in one of the secondary area newspapers in an article titled "School Board candidacies take shape." The first paragraph follows a quoted statement from one of the board members who had decided not to run again (note: His candidacy was not at stake as he spoke.):

> The most important issue, however, is support of Superintendent Dr. [Kelly], who [board member] feels is moving the district in the right direction. Even recent revelations of financial problems show that [Kelly] is cleaning up previous financial problems, he said.
>
> "If they hadn't come out, that would mean we were either whitewashing it or we were in denial that there were problems in the district," [board member] said. "It is hard for the public to realize that. There isn't a real sense of history among the general population about how these things came to be the way they are."
>
> Cooperation with city and county government and work force development programs will be [another board member who will run again]'s main campaign issues, but school overcrowding, construction funding and financial accountability will obviously be hot issues, he said.
>
> [Board member who will run again] hopes voters will remember that changing the way the district operates is not going to happen easily or quickly.
>
> "We are going to turn stones over that are not pretty, but that is not going to dissuade me from continuing to look under every rock so that we can make sure that the inadequate funds for education are spent wisely," she said." (January 23, 1998, p.1)

This article made it clear to me that the board of education was supportive of Dr. Kelly's work in the district even when it meant "telling all" about skeletons discovered in various closets.

Finally, returning to the comments of the district administrator in charge of communications—he ended his conversation with me by stating, "Dr. [Kelly] is resistant to manipulation and so grounded in her sense of self and in her beliefs," that she will continue to do what is right.

USEFUL FINDINGS FOR ADMINISTRATORS AND EDUCATORS

This case study had several findings that promise to be instructive:

1. The woman superintendent's definition and use of power—"power with/to"—permeated her response to the media. She chose to use power in collaborative ways. She constantly convened and met with the representative bodies of the large community in an effort to unify and recognize all voices, the voices of those misrepresented, to construct additional more fully representative official knowledge about the community and its schools.
2. All representatives of the community and school district in this single-case

study agreed that the media misrepresented them, their school district, and their superintendent.

3. There was a sense of helplessness, a true loss of the "voice" of everyone because the media took an oppressively dominant position of power in the community studied. The community, school district, and superintendent were "objectified" by the press (hooks, 1989).

4. Those representatives of the community at large (1.3 million people) expected the superintendent to "fix" the schools for the community in spite of the problems the school district and the superintendent faced due to the press.

5. Representatives of the community and the school district in the study agreed that the negative press representation of the school district was damaging to the education and welfare of the children in the district, as well as to the economic health of the community.

6. Through a philosophy of power as shared, Dr. Kelly was able to negotiate spaces where she and others could begin to represent the school district in a more positive light. Moving without the typical public relations solutions, she advanced beliefs that accepted even the most negative of adversaries—the *Newspaper*. With these beliefs as foundation, district personnel and board of education members took action to "do the right thing" and to "tell all." And as the press began to see consistent action, their attention began to turn elsewhere.

7. The problem of this negative press was not "fixed" even though the district was experiencing some relief. This particular press just moved on to other targets and, indeed, turned its attention back on the school district at times, as can be seen in the case of the referendum. To more fully change the practices of the *Newspaper* would take an innovative, courageous, and comprehensive community-wide effort. Dr. Kelly was well aware of this fact, as were other people in the school district. They believed that they could never become self-satisfied even though the school district and thus, the community was beginning to have space to represent itself in a more balanced way.

8. The study outcome suggests that the superintendent's response to the press was effective, in large part, because her concept of power was "with/to" work with others to accomplish goals. This conception was the foundation for a philosophy of inclusive action—on the part of the superintendent and the district—that accepted rather than attacked the adversarial press.

9. Furthermore, the study outcome indicates that all superintendents, administrators, and educators need the skills necessary to help communities find ways for individual and collective self-representations in order that public schools and communities have fair opportunities to be visible, respected, and considered legitimate. Such work requires an understanding of the politics of representation and the nature of collaborative, shared power in order that the relationship between the public schools and the media can be positively negotiated.

FINAL EXERCISES FOR STUDENTS

1. Compare and contrast your own action plans to the actual events in the case.
2. Describe how such a case would look in your district. How would it be different? alike?
3. Do you have stories about the media and the public schools that you could share with classmates?
4. What ideas do you have for impacting or changing the current negative attitude of the media toward public education? Who would you involve in making your ideas work?

REFERENCES

Clegg, S. (1989). *Frameworks of Power.* London: Sage.

Ellsworth, E. (1994). "Representation, Self-Representation, and the Meanings of Difference: Questions for Educators." In R. M. Martusewicz and W. M. Reynolds (Eds.), *Inside Out: Contemporary Critical Perspective in Education* (pp. 99–108). Mahwah, NJ: Erlbaum.

Follett, M. P. (1942). *Creative Experience.* New York: Longmans, Green.

Gans, H. J. (1980). *Deciding What's News.* New York: Vintage

Hartsock, N. (1981). "Political Change: Two Perspectives on Power." In C. Bunch (Ed.), *Building Feminist Theory: Essays from Quest.* New York: Longman.

hooks, b. (1989). *Talking Back: Thinking Feminists, Thinking Black.* Boston, MA: South End Press.

Kaplan, G. R. (1992). *Images of Education: The Mass Media's Version of America's Schools.* Washington, D.C.: Institute for Educational Leadership.

Sarason, D. B. (1990). *The Predictable Failure of Educational Reform: Can We Change Course before It's Too Late?* San Francisco: Jossey-Bass.

6

Education Apolitical? Don't Bet on It!

William G. Cunningham

You are the superintendent of the Jefferson School Division. Your renewal team is made up of school board members, central office staff, principals, PTA members, and a few teachers. You have formed this vertical team to assist with a new curriculum that you want to develop and test in two high schools and, most important, to lay a quality foundation for Jefferson's renewal efforts. The board expects to see "results" over the next three-year period, which coincides with the length remaining on your superintendent contract. The board has established a number of goals for you and the committee. The four most prominent of these goals are as follows:

- To implement curriculum and instructional improvements that better meet the needs of students as they move forward to take on job and community roles and/or to attend universities
- To finalize implementation plans for the high school renewal effort
- To gain necessary support to be able to give renewal plans the maximum chance for success
- To revitalize the public image of the school district

The previous superintendent, working with the board, had developed the following mission statement:

The Jefferson City School District believes each student is unique and can learn. The district's mission is to provide instruction, programs, strategies, and challenges in a caring, positive learning environment. Each student will be prepared to meet the challenges of our changing global society as a critical, integrated thinker, a lifelong learner, and a responsible, contributing, productive citizen.

However, the board has changed recently because "they were unable to make progress on meeting the challenges the mission prescribed," and they replaced the previous superintendent who was forced to retire and is now living in a neighboring community. The new board supports the existing mission statement and is particularly interested in developing critical thinkers who understand issues from "complex and multiple perspectives." The call is to prepare Jefferson schools to meet the many challenges that lie ahead. Support was growing for an integrated curriculum to connect traditional disciplines and make applications across content areas.

You and your team have the following challenges:

- To move key people within the district toward the new interdisciplinary curriculum proposed for implementation within Franklin and Hamilton High Schools
- To build a quality foundation for both high schools so as to maximize the probability of success for the renewal effort
- To lay out a general renewal plan for the short- and long-term implementation efforts
- To gain the confidence and the support of the internal and external community regarding their public school system

THE COMMUNITY

Jefferson City is a changing suburban city of approximately three hundred thousand people on the outskirts of a large urban center that is in the process of undergoing major urban renewal. Its economy has been based primarily on one Fortune 500 company located within the city, as well as service, tourism, and the entertainment industry. A number of prominent executives and doctors have established residence in Jefferson City to avoid urban decay; however, this trend has shifted as a number of the more powerful and wealthy community figures have either moved back to the city center or to new, more exclusive self-contained communities in the surrounding rural areas. Mass transit seems to have accelerated the exodus; as a result, the aging suburban community is itself beginning to show signs of decline. Certainly, the community is becoming more diverse in almost every way. The rapid changes have caused a dilution of traditional power structures within the community. The small group of powerful individuals who once had a strong influence on the area's politics and leadership is now giving way to a broader more complex leadership structure.

The community is trying to figure out ways of broadening existing leadership while including representation from the diverse groups. The current emphasis within the city is to lower barriers to communication and understanding, identify opportunities for broader involvement, expand the pool of civic leaders, and facilitate a shared vision among the diverse populations within the community. The local chamber of commerce has come to accept their dilution of power and are taking a leading role in trying to broaden the leadership base. The Coalition of Civic Organizations was created a year ago to gain more power for grassroots leaders. A citywide development corporation was formed to address problems of economic decline and to propose new ideas for economic development. There are also foundations, a small college, churches, real estate and building associations, women's groups, and others who are becoming more vocal regarding the community's future. The city council has begun to shift its role from directing and controlling to guiding, facilitating, supporting and coordinating the efforts of other groups. More than half of the residents recognize that the city must act strategically, encourage innovation and risk taking, and focus attention and effort on critical issues.

There is, however, still an element that wants the city to remain as it was thirty years ago. As of yet, no ongoing dialogue is apparent, and factions often work against and counter to one another, using subterfuge and any other means to influence outcomes. Unless methods are found to adapt to changed and changing environments, the city's future may be less than optimal. The former mayor stated, "There needs to be a recognition that we've got to evolve into a broader leadership base to address community problems." The chairman of the school board and a friend of the previous mayor concurred: "What happens many times in leadership is that quite a few of our citizens feel left out. We're trying to be more inclusive."

THE DISTRICT

Total enrollment in the Jefferson City public school district is fifty-seven thousand students. The district includes a central administration, a nine-member school board, fifty-five elementary schools, eleven middle schools, and nine high schools. The district students' ethnic background has been shifting to a much more diverse population, composed of 55% white, 28% black, 8% Hispanic, 5% Asian, and 4% other. Over 60% of the students' parents are college educated. Students seemed to be very knowledgeable but immature; many believe this to be the cause of a significant increase in discipline problems. Although the district had once been considered one of the best in the state, it had been on the decline for many years and was now only slightly above average in terms of its test scores. The president of the chamber of commerce recently stated, "Our schools do not seem up to the task of producing graduates who can handle the more complex and demanding roles of our industry and commerce. Ultimately, the burden of change rests with our schools, and something has to be done soon." In fact, the previous superintendent, who was very popular within the community, was pressured to retire early and against his wishes because he had maintained the status quo for too long.

Nothing much had changed in Jefferson schools for over twenty years even though everything around them underwent massive change. The overall program has been described as very conservative and very traditional. Technology is available but was primarily a separate entity, with students being given time to go to computer labs to improve their skills. The high schools are completely departmentalized by discipline. Faculty members are assigned to a department and only teach courses offered by the department. Each department has a chairperson who is given a great deal of autonomy. The departments seldom ever communicate with one another and as a result are quite different in almost every aspect. Teachers stay in the same room all day, and students change classrooms every fifty minutes. There are six periods a day (one free period) and a lunch break. Almost all other aspects of the program vary depending on the department. Principals do have brief department chair meetings primarily to share information. One board member, who was a strong proponent for replacing the past superintendent, stated, "Unless education adopts and adapts to new expectations, our schools stand to lose their relevance to the needs of society." She went on to say, "Many of us feel mobilized and empowered to continuously improve our schools and somehow our superintendent is paralyzed. There is an emerging consensus that to turn our schools around requires a fundamental bone-jarring revolution in the status quo." The superintendent suggested that this may not be a widely held view, but he was asked to retire by the end of the year.

The procedures used to select you, the new superintendent of schools, stressed school law, school administration, and school finance; however, they also required an individual with vision who could plan strategically and work with the community and existing staff to continuously improve the schools. The expectation was for a superintendent who would help the district rethink education and to create entirely new, more effective approaches. You were hired because you were perceived as "a person who could provide the needed leadership for improved, more relevant education while at the same time bridging the gaps that have grown between the diverse populations." During your interview you stated, "Students need to think strategically, to create visions, learn in a changing environment, connect knowledge to authentic problems, build multidisciplinary perspectives, understand diverse contexts, and collaborate both locally and globally using technology." You were told that your ability to see a new future for the schools weighted heavily on your selection. However, you were also aware when you first arrived that there was a sense of great concern among parents, teachers, and older, powerful community members as to what you might do. An assistant superintendent who had been hired by the previous superintendent told you early in your first year "you will need everyone's support if any efforts at reform are to succeed."

The renewal team is made up of you, school board members, a new assistant superintendent for curriculum and instruction that you hired, the assistant superintendent for finance, director(s), coordinator(s), high school principal(s) (the two experimental high schools), assistant principal(s), teacher(s), and the PTA president(s) from the schools. This group works as a vertical team. Team members' participation is based on the quality of information provided and not on position power. A professional facilitator from the local university facilitated all team meetings, and a skilled secretary recorded minutes. It was hoped that this vertical team would strengthen the connections among people at all levels within the organization. It would support the exchange of information regarding needed curriculum and instructional reform.

A principal at one of the high schools had expressed concern that the school system had too many groups involved and should not be political. A seasoned assistant superintendent of over twenty years stated, "Schools not political? Don't bet on it! The myth of apolitical schools has gotten more than one administrator in trouble in this school district. Schools touch many people's lives, are very visible, and require considerable resources. The competing demands are being debated among a number of powerful groups." She went on to say, "The powerless will have to learn how to gain power if they want their voices to be heard."

Team members were provided common literature regarding possible innovations and asked to discuss it with others prior to coming to meetings. You have stressed that "position differences must disappear as the group begins to care about what is best for the children and appreciate each others points of view."

The committee was charged with looking into the possibility of two experimental interdisciplinary programs at the local high schools. The superintendent had received tentative approval to investigate possibilities and to move toward implementation at Franklin and Hamilton High Schools. These two schools were located in upper-middle-class neighborhoods. There seemed to be support in these two communities for greater interconnectedness within the curriculum especially by residents who were members of the chamber of commerce and civic leagues.

Any subject is always related to many other subjects and issues, and the curriculum and instruction should be designed to represent this interrelatedness. The idea was to figure ways by which more than one discipline could be used by students to examine an authentic theme, issue, problem, topic, or experience. Fragmentation of subject matter and schedules were to be reduced or eliminated. Showing how subject areas relate along with the relevance of the curriculum was to be stressed. Previous attempts at interdisciplinary curriculum had been unsuccessful; however, there is research that stresses the benefits of this approach. Many citizens believe it is more relevant to the world in which students live. The board had stressed that this approach should not replace the discipline field approach but should show how disciplines are mutually supportive.

Everyone on the reform team has been asked to read J. M. Palmer's (1991) "Planning Wheels Turn Curriculum Around" prior to the next meeting. Table 6.1 provides an example of how planning wheels can be used to think through interdisciplinary curriculum. A consultant stated that, "The ideal curriculum is one in which the maximum coherence is achieved and segmentation is minimized." The planning wheel provides a flexible vehicle for addressing the need to "get started" making connections. Table 6.1 relates an environmental topic, acid rain, to the major subject/discipline areas so that all subjects are connected by this topic. The planning wheel pulls subjects together to focus on a common topic for a given period of time. If successful, eventually this approach can be expanded to other high schools.

Table 6.1   Acid Rain Planning Wheel

Grade 9

Essential Questions
1. What is acid rain?
2. How does it occur?
3. How has acid rain impacted society?
4. What can be done to reduce or eliminate acid rain?

Science
- Define acid rain. Collect water samples from school or community site. Analyze samples for the acids content. Report results to health dept.

Social Studies
- Collect news and magazine articles
- Investigate possible solutions to the problem of U.S. factories causing acid rain to fall in Canada
- Generate ways people could help reduce the causes of acid rain.

Mathematics
- Compile data from surveys and experiments
- Analyze, graph, and interpret data to draw conclusions about acid rain.

ACID RAIN

Language Arts/Reading
- Develop questions in order to conduct a survey of public awareness and attitudes toward acid rain.
- Write letters to public officials requesting action on the acid rain issues.
- Create stories about Earth in the year 2050 if the acid rain problems continue as they are at present.

Art
- Draw editorial cartoons based on the acid rain issue.
- Design and initiate a poster campaign.
- Create illustrations of Earth in the year 2050 if the acid rain problems continue as they are at present.

Health/Physical Education
- Discuss possible health problems caused by acid rain.

Computer-Related Instruction
- Use telecommunications on the computer, through a National Geographic Society unit called KidsNet, to access current acid rain data from all over the country and the world. Input student data collected from the school site.

Source: Glascock, R. O., and Mitchell, E. H. (1990). *A Curriculum Connections Model. ASCD for the Middle Grades.* Baltimore: Maryland State Department of Education. Association for Supervision and Curriculum Development

TEACHERS

The average age of the high school teaching staff is thirty-eight. Thirty percent of the teachers are black, 65% are white, and the remainder represents a number of other races and cultures. Approximately 70% of the teachers are female. They teach for five fifty-minute classes, and they have a free period and a lunch break. Historically, Jefferson teachers stress the importance of discretion in discussing schools, programs, and colleagues with others, within or outside the schools. Loyalty to the principal, school division, and the superintendent has always been demanded. In this way, teachers have an important public relations role to play in building the image of the school. There were, however, visible signs of stress among teachers regarding the reform agenda. Absenteeism, complaining, resistance, and rumors were all on the increase; however, the school culture kept most from openly discussing any type of concerns.

The teachers were satisfied with the existing curriculum and school structure even though they felt pressure to revise, improve, and update it. They had always supported the previous superintendent because renewal and time-consuming development was not really part of the culture and "he had pretty much left us alone." There was a complacency that the teachers did not like but had grown to accept as part of the job. They were very comfortable with what and how they taught even if they were slowly getting bored with it all and were no longer sure it was relevant. They recognized that the times were calling for new approaches and new methods of instruction, particularly with the "explosion of information," but they did not see any strong support beyond conflicting rhetoric. The state's new testing program seemed to support the traditional approaches and further confused the teachers as to what needed to be done to reform education. They also had felt powerless regarding needed reforms and had no authority to make any changes.

They had serious doubts about any reforms being successful and were aware of the legacy of failed reforms that had occurred throughout the county. They had taken pride in the fact that they were not part of that "reform mess" and had stuck to the "tried and true" methods. They did not want their roles or responsibilities restructured and were questioning "whether or not we will like the results." They were very concerned about the time it would take to restructure the curriculum, to learn new skills and roles, and to prepare lessons and teach under a new revised approach. This particularly seemed ill advised since no one could be sure that the new approach would in fact be better than what was already in place.

They, in fact, had been defending the schools and the existing programs for many years and could see no reason to change now. The teachers at the two high schools selected for experimentation were probably slightly more open to reform; however, they too shared many of the same concerns held by the majority of teachers in the district. They did believe that being selected to participate in this first wave of reform would enhance their value to the district. One of the growing concerns was whether they would be able to be effective in implementing new instructional approaches and what would happen to them if they were not. Would they be penalized?

BUSINESS AND COMMERCE

The local business and commerce communities were very concerned that Jefferson City students were not being prepared to be successful at the university level or in the world of work. They had been seriously hurt by economic decline, unemployment, and the need for massive retraining of new employees. Wages in the city had been losing ground and they were unable to attract technology-related business because of a growing concern about the ability of the workforce and the quality of the schools. The factory workers were now competing against third world countries, and the jobs were being shifted to less expensive labor markets. There was a need for more complex work and the high level of expertise to succeed in these industries. The local community was very concerned that the schools were not preparing students for this new more demanding world of work.

The demand was for problem solving, reasoning, analyzing, developing inferential skills, advancing topics, thinking strategically, and building knowledge. It also required collaborative work, interpersonal skills, teamwork, and vision. Students also needed a strong understanding of technology including access to the Internet, information processing, and active learning using new technology. The call was for employees who can work together. There was a strong concern that subject/disciplines—and later professionals—remained in relative isolation from one another even as businesses faced more serious interconnected problems. There was an important need to link disciplines and work together if the economic base was to be revitalized. The chairperson of the "Forward Jefferson City" committee stated, "The time is upon us when we must learn to work together to provide multidisciplinary approaches to our businesses and communities. This must begin with our schools." The theme was to develop linkages among the disciplines along with coordinated and integrated approaches to meet the complex multidisciplinary problems now being confronted. Students must learn how each of the various disciplines contributes to the future success of business and communities by validating how interconnected the disciplines are in the authentic problems people face. The chairperson for Forward Jefferson City went on to state, "One of the greatest city needs is to have workers who can work together to solve problems and take needed actions to improve our business and our community. We are in danger of becoming a community of low-skilled, low-wage, underclass citizens. The isolation of disciplines in the face of problems requiring multidisciplinary solutions is a serious cause of this problem."

PARENTS

The parents of the students, who have middle- to upper-middle-class backgrounds, have incomes that have not been keeping pace with national trends; a number have lost their jobs owing to technological advances and more demanding expectations. There is a paradox in the views expressed by parents in that they agree with the demands that business and commerce are placing on education but they don't think its needed at their children's school. As a result, they are not generally in favor of the proposed changes, "whatever they are," and are not receptive to the "intrusion" of "new ideas" in the classroom which will make their children "guinea pigs." They are concerned that multidisciplinary approaches may overwhelm and confuse their children and thrust them into real-world situations for which they are not prepared. They expressed concern that this might result in decreased performance and adverse emotional effects. The president of the PTA at Franklin High School stated, "Our children need time to gain skills in each discipline, to learn values, and to begin to form a sense of their own identities. Our adolescents need time to develop their personalities, decide on their future careers, and mature physically and emotionally before they face the complexity of authentic problems and the need to integrate all that they have learned."

Unanimity is lacking among parents, and the past school board elections resulted in numerous heated debates over many issues, with school reform at the top of the list. Changes in the community had brought many newcomers to the area who were very supportive of the position of the business and community leaders. These so-called "outsiders" had brought new ideas and ways of doing things and had influenced others who were longtime residents. There were many conflicts among the residents of the community, and the school board elections had evolved into an ideological battleground. The school board president confided in you, "The previous superintendent was unable to get a handle on conflicting views about how schools should respond and was unable to play a mediating leadership role. He seemed unable to avoid painful, ineffective arguments. He did not have the discipline to stay away from distracting arguments and to provide a clear vision for future actions." Some had suggested that "destructive forces had destroyed relationships and cohesiveness." It was shortly after the election that the previous superintendent resigned and you were hired.

Your predecessor congratulated you but warned about the growing fragmentation within the community:

> I have built a strong administrative staff, but the community seemed to abandon us. We have always gone "by the book," but now everyone seems to want special treatment or changes to meet their ideological beliefs. I resisted these pressures, but that is what probably cost me my job. I am leaving knowing I did what is best for children and teachers. If you don't follow the manual, you better have good reason why you didn't, and you better never take anyone's support for granted. Don't get me wrong,

I understand the demands for reform, but no one really knows what they want, and they all seem to disagree. It doesn't take very long until you look back and realize you have little support for any change you decide to make.

He ended by offering assistance to you and explaining he is retired and in the area so don't hesitate to call on him. His grandchildren attend schools in the district.

STUDENTS AND SCHOOLS

The students at Franklin and Hamilton High Schools are slightly more affluent than the students in five of the other high schools and significantly more affluent than the students in two other high schools. Two thousand nine hundred students attend Franklin, and 2,200 students attend Hamilton High School in grades 9–12. Both schools are valued at approximately $10.5 million and are on large lots with basketball courts, softball diamonds, tracks, and so forth. There are at least three computers in every classroom and eleven computer labs in each of the schools. The rooms are wired for telephones and the Internet. Almost 70% of the students ride school buses to school. Student attendance, which had been steadily increasing in the past, has been declining slightly over the past three years. The dropout rate has been increasing slightly and is now about 6%. Eighty-two percent of all students were promoted. Honor roll statistics have also risen to 40%. Special education programs have expanded consistently since the opening of the buildings approximately fifty years ago. Scores on standardized tests are on the decline; however, the schools' averages are both slightly above the state average.

Little to no lasting changes have been made to the curriculum over the past fifteen years, even though complaints about both the curricular and instructional programs are at an all-time high. The key theme from both students and their parents is a "lack of relevance." There is also concern that there is too much structure at a time when students want to be treated more as adults. The schools are totally departmentalized with faculty members seldom seeing or talking to faculty in other departments and only teaching courses offered in their department. Department chairpersons are given considerable autonomy and seldom meet except for the exchange of information. As a result, the departments are all quite different in almost every way.

Services offered to students within the building have increased significantly over the last five years. Students tend to be more interested in cocurricular activities and athletics than academics. They describe their classes as outdated and boring. A recent survey of students' attitudes suggested that lessons are not interesting or thought-provoking, there was a lack of positive reinforcement and order in the classroom, and it was difficult to see the usefulness of what was being taught. Students feel that they don't have enough time to work on significant projects and that they are expected to memorize too much meaningless information. They feel that their parents and the community are concerned about the present quality of their education and that causes them some anxiety. Students seldom discuss their concerns within the classroom or the school. Students seem to lack motivation and the community's confusion regarding schools and teachers, and the curriculum seems to be a contributing factor. Many students have directed their energies toward the expanding set of extracurricular and service activities.

Of particular concern was a fight that occurred following a Franklin/Booker T. Washington basketball game at Booker T. Students from both schools became involved in a loud scuffle after the game. Nearby residents at a number of schools had been complaining about noise and rowdiness on school grounds, particularly after dusk. Residents regularly called the police, stating that fifty to a hundred people were there at a time. They suggested that the school grounds had become a meeting place for drinking, listening to music, and gang-related activities. The rowdiness, profanity, and fighting after the game unified the residents who were demanding that the city council and school board do something about this problem. Thirty-five families had signed a letter of complaint and sent it to you. There was a concern that this was a sign of broader problems within the school and community. One student said, "I felt real sad. There is nothing to do, no one cares about us, and now they want to take away our basketball and other athletics." One neighbor called and told you that the disturbance after the game was gang related and he thought he had seen a gun. This was especially disturbing because of one of Booker T. Washington's students had been arrested and jailed in connection with a drive-by shooting near one of the high schools. Special charges are pending. The schools and students were now under even a closer media and community scrutiny.

You have been sensing a high level of distress in both the schools and the community, and this situation was sure to add to it. Some had already begun to discuss extreme measures to restore "law and order" and protect the students. There was a sense of disequilibrium that seemed to disrupt the normal flow of daily instruction, creating uncertainty, fear, and emotional turmoil at a number of school sites. The superintendent felt that the principals lacked training in dealing with such turmoil, and the general practice seemed to be "sweep it under the rug." You had been warned by a superintendent in the surrounding area, "Don't let the urgent replace the important. Quick fixes most often set a course for future crisis."

You as superintendent can sense that conditions are much worse than you had realized when you accepted this job. It seems like everyone's concerns are escalating in intensity. The system is coming under increased media and community scrutiny. Everyone seems to be concerned about students and their schools. The public image of the school district is not good. The conditions have actually reached a point where they are interfering with the normal operation of the school district and several of the schools. Little planning is under way on how to deal with any type of crisis. The past administration seems to have ignored the initial signs of problems, and now that they have increased, no one—from the classroom teacher to the school board—was prepared to deal with them. There is not even a list of people to contact, important emergency telephone numbers, or procedures for handling media representatives. The previous superintendent and board members who were recently replaced have lost credibility, and that, along with a lack of communication, has created an atmosphere of suspicion.

PROBLEM AND ACTIVITIES GUIDE

The problem as presented here is to develop a short- and long-range strategic plan for implementing needed reforms within the Jefferson School District while continuing to run an effective educational program. The focus should be on the implementation of districtwide reform starting at Franklin and Hamilton High Schools. You should include how the plans will be developed, how they will be implemented, and how they will be evaluated. You must consider all the factors presented and make needed deductions on how to approach the development and implementation effort. Be careful not to overlook any of the intricacies of this challenging situation. There is some polarization in regard to diverse opinions that is to be addressed as part of the solution, and the culture is not conducive to the planning and implementation process.

A school renewal team was appointed to study the entire situation and assist you with the responsibility for identifying an approach that will have the greatest probability of success in your school division. You may use this team in any way you wish. Your final plan should include a report of all activities including gathering information, talking to community and staff, making presentations, conducting workshops, revising curriculum, assigning responsibility, and working with others. You should make all your decisions based on how you would handle this situation if you were the superintendent of a real school district like the one described. You should then record the decision and relate it to the development and implementation effort. Record the titles of individuals or groups that will be involved. Present your plan in chronological order showing the sequence and scope of each planned activity. Discuss and record information as you go along.

LEARNING OBJECTIVES

- Establishing policies and procedures for selecting curricular and instructional programs and materials and for reviewing them when they are challenged
- Obtaining needed support for curricular and instructional practices and materials used in reforming education
- Identifying those who can help in developing and implementing successful school reforms
- Building credibility into your proposal

- Establishing needed communication networks
- Understanding what's going on, being on top of details, and seeing the big picture
- Making effective well-supported decisions from a legal, policy, political, and practical perspective

GUIDING QUESTIONS

There is a hierarchical structure to the following nine questions in that they begin with general strategies, preparation, and planning and move toward detailed operational analysis and planning. In this way, each response becomes a more detailed subset related to preceding responses.

1. How can you build a solid political base to support school reform and help in times of future crisis?
2. What types of concerns are most likely to occur at each stage in the development and implementation process?
3. What needs will occur at each of the different stages of the development and implementation process?
4. What will be the role of the various groups and/or people involved?
5. Briefly outline each of the stages in your development and implementation process.
6. What will your decision-making process and strategy be? Who will be involved at each stage?
7. How important is the signed letter of complaint from residents living near the high schools and how will you approach this matter?
8. What is your short- and long-term plan of action at each stage? Include your rationale.
9. How will your plans restore equilibrium in this particular situation?

PRODUCT SPECIFICATIONS

As the superintendent, ending your first year in Jefferson School District, you are expected to address the demand for school reform at the high school level while supporting the smooth operation of the school system. You are asked to develop a short- and long-term strategic plan of action for developing and implementing needed high school reforms. The short-term plan should focus on experimentation at Franklin and Hamilton High Schools, with the long-term plan expanding to all high schools within the district. You should stress how the plans will be developed and implemented. They should include the names of groups and specific jobholders that will need to be involved and the rationale for their involvement. The plan should be organized in chronological order showing the sequence, scope, and purpose/goal of each activity within the action plan. You should also briefly describe the process and rationale regarding the final recommendations. You are expected to provide this complete written report and oral overview to the board of education at a future meeting. You have been asked to set the date as to when you will be prepared to address the board on the reform issues.

The roles of the reform team are to mirror the constituents that they represent. They should keep the context and the attitudes of those they represent in mind when participating. A sampling of the membership of the reform team will be asked to discuss and comment on your plan of action at the board of education meeting when you present the school reform package. Team members are expected to complete an assessment of the plan presented and why it would or would not be successful. They might also discuss what they believe would be needed to result in successful school reform. All participants should provide a reflective essay on what they learned from this experience.

You as superintendent and/or members of the reform team are expected to obtain all additional materials that might be needed to address this assignment.

REFERENCES

Carter, G. R., and Cunningham, W. G. (1997). *The American School Superintendent: Leading in an Age of Pressure.* San Francisco: Jossey-Bass.

Cunningham, W. (September/October, 1997). "Are You Ready for 21st Century Schools?" *The High School Magazine.*

Cunningham, W. G., and Cordeiro, P. A. (2000). *Educational Administration: A Problem-Based Approach.* Boston: Allyn & Bacon.

Cunningham, W. G., and Gresso, D.W. (1993). *Cultural Leadership: The Culture of Excellence in Education.* Boston: Allyn and Bacon.

Darling-Hammond, L. (1992). "Reframing the School Reforms Agenda." *School Administrator* 4(9): 22–27.

Fullan, M. (1997). *What's Worth Fighting for in the Principalship.* New York: Teachers College Press.

Graves, Bill. (1992, April). "The Pressure Group Cooker." *School Administrator.*

Gurskey, T. R., and Peterson, K. D. (December 1995/January 1996). "The Road to Classroom Change." *Educational Leadership.*

Heifetz, R.A. (1994). *Leading without Easy Answers.* Cambridge, MA: Harvard University Press.

Howelett, Patricia. (January 1993). "Politics Comes to School." *Executive Educator.*

Jacobs, H. H. (October, 1991). "Planning for Curriculum Integration." *Educational Leadership* 49: 27–28.

Morris, Christine. (December, 1992). "Pressure Groups and the Politics of Education," *Updating School Board Policies* 23: 9. (A publication of the National School Board Association.)

Murphy, J., and Hallinger, P. (Eds.). (1993). *Restructuring Schooling: Learning from On-going Efforts*. Newbury Park, CA: Courier.

Palmer, J. M. (October, 1991). "Planning Wheels Turn Curriculum Around." *Educational Leadership* 49: 61–65.

Schlechly, P. C. (1997). *Inventing Better Schools*. San Francisco: Jossey-Bass.

Short, P. M., and Greer, J. T. (1997). *Leadership in Empowered Schools*. Upper Saddle River, NJ: Merrill/Prentice Hall.

———. (October 27, 1997). "What Makes a Good School: Special Report." *Time* 150: 17.

7

Hard Word Makes Good Luck:
A Profile of Success

Nadyne Guzmán and Al Ramirez

"Congratulations, you've just been named captain of the *Titanic*." That's how the newly appointed superintendent of schools for El Paso County School District 11 in Colorado Springs, Colorado, must have felt after he accepted the job in 1987 and got his first close look at the school district from the captain's chair. His application and paperwork were flawless, his interview went great, and he got strong ratings from stakeholder groups involved in the selection process. He had done his homework, researched the district, and asked all the right questions before signing his contract. Kenneth Stephen Burnley, Ph.D., and the board had a "marriage made in heaven"— or so it seemed.

This case study is based on the experiences of Burnley in his eleven years as superintendent of schools in this Colorado district. It is a testament to a school leader who persevered in the face of major adversities. It is the story of success where failure was imminent. It is a lesson about the power of hard work, intelligence, commitment, and leadership.

CHAOS AND DENIAL: TAKING CHARGE

Ken Burnley soon found out that the magnitude of problems facing School District 11 were much larger and more entrenched than he had been led to believe. These problems included several historical and long-standing issues, serious financial problems, and a traditional lack of community support that was beginning to turn into hostility. Any one of these concern areas could sink a leader in a short time. In fact, Burnley was the seventh superintendent in eleven years. Many fully expected that he would be gone in no time. Even the "good ol' boys" in the administrators

97

association wrote him off before he got started; their knock on Burnley was that he would "blow in, blow hard, and blow out."

The school district was like the "grand lady" who had lost her looks and money or the star athlete who stayed on for one too many seasons. Many in the organization—including staff, administrators, parents, key community leaders, and school board members—were living with the delusions of past glory, when the district had built its international reputation as being on the cutting edge of public education. However, times were tough now, and few were willing, able, or empowered to pull the district out of its malaise. The decline within this district had built up over many years. It was characterized as having the traditionally adversarial relationship with the local teachers' association, a central office that was inefficient and ineffective, a system built on seniority and friendship with little regard for qualifications or competence, and poor financial practices that threatened the district's survival.

The financial situation in the school district was at a crisis point. This was one of the biggest bombshells Burnley faced when he walked in the door. The board told him, when he inquired about the financial condition of the school district during the interview stage, that the district had a $1 million deficit. Not good, but an amount that could be covered in an operating budget of $98 million. When he looked into the budget situation, he discovered that the budget gap was not $1 million as he had been told but $12 million!

If the $12 million budget deficit were not enough, Burnley got more bad news when he learned that the state of Colorado had just adopted a new school finance formula that grouped school districts by community characteristics, and it had categorized School District 11 improperly. Under the new school finance act, the school district faced several years of declining revenue from the state. When the legislature moved to realign the state finance act, which took place well before Burnley's arrival, no one from School District 11 was at the state house to protect the school district's interests. As a result, the district was assigned a disadvantageous position in the funding scheme.

The denial about the slippage that had taken place in the district was not limited to the staff. The community, at least among most longtime residents, believed the district was still in its glory days. Problems, if any, were the fault of the staff or the board. Most residents were happy with their schools—the only thing needing to be fixed were the schools across town. The status quo was, to them, a desirable state.

Colorado Springs is regarded as one of the more politically conservative cities in Colorado and therefore the nation. It is the home of Colorado's tax limitation citizen initiative; it has five major military installations in the area and is a highly desirable retirement community. The manifestation of these demographics meant Ken Burnley faced a very fiscally stingy community. A bond levy had not passed in the school district for twenty years, neither for operations nor for capital projects. Things looked okay. Buildings were still in good repair and the buses were running; so what was the problem?

To compound all of this chaos and denial about the school district, Burnley also knew that few in the organization understood or cared about the social, political, demographic, and economic changes taking place in the broader society, changes that would have a major impact on the organization. He understood that these changes would affect the education of all children, even those not yet in school. He understood too that changes were needed in the district to accomplish several basic objectives: meet the immediate fiscal and human resource challenges in the district; refocus the district toward the future; create a mission-driven organization; gain the financial resources needed to get the job done; and, above all, build an every improving quality of education for students.

KEY INGREDIENTS FOR SUCCESS

The remarkable turnaround of District 11 happened because of a lot of hard work and intelligence. Burnley never relied on luck to bail out the district. He understood that, while times were tough for the school district and the undertaking needed to turn things around was extensive, he needed to apply good management techniques and be a leader for the district. He knew that his work ethic and history of working hard to reach goals would be necessary to lead the district toward success. His approach was at once both subtle and direct.

Ken saw that what was most lacking in the district was leadership. It was a lack of leadership that had allowed the district to drift into the state that it was in, with budget problems, communications problems, and community concerns. He never lost sight of the fact that he was the seventh person to assume the superintendent's chair in little more than a decade. He determined that good leadership was the paramount ingredient for success and essential to breaking the inertia in the system.

Consistent with his philosophy of good management and of modeling good leadership, Burnley insisted that all new positions or vacancies, if they were to be filled, would be filled by the best talent available. He believed (and does to this day) that management is getting things done through others and to get them done right you need the right people in place. For a district that historically valued other criteria for appointments and promotions, this was a new concept. Professional search firms were engaged to seek candidates for key positions and to aggressively recruit talent. Burnley's admonition to the "head hunters" as they conducted their nationwide searches was "get me the best."

From day one, Burnley was evaluating the school district. He went through every major and minor system in the district, including finance and budget, staffing and personnel, buildings and grounds, community relations, transportation, curriculum, and assessment. Beyond each major system, he delved into the subsystems and processes that supported the major systems. In addition, he met and talked with the individuals responsible for each system or process. As a result of this analysis of the district, Burnley formed a comprehensive picture of the school district and its current state of affairs. He learned about key weaknesses and areas of strengths in the district. This helped him formulate his plan of attack; it helped prioritize problems (crises, in reality); it allowed Burnley to be strategic about using available resources.

One remnant of the organizational culture Burnley moved to overcome quickly was the blind pursuit of personal gain within the bureaucratic structure of the school district. As the leader of the district, Burnley wanted to be sure he had team players in place to take on the difficult tasks ahead. Rogue administrators and petty political despots could not be counted on during the tough transition period ahead. Their history had been to obstruct and undermine any effort that threatened to put them out or diminish their personal power in the organization. Burnley was very forthright on this issue. He let it be known that team play was a job requirement and those who were unwilling or incapable of joining the team were encouraged to leave. Every effort would be made to help these folks find employment in other organizations. All members of the District 11 staff were to be team players. Under the old organizational culture what mattered was "who you knew." Burnley insisted that what really mattered is "what you can do." To the amazement and consternation of many, hiring practices started to reflect this new philosophy.

Consistent with the team orientation, Burnley worked hard to make sure everyone knew that any progress made or effort attempted was by and for the team. His constant message to the organization and the outside community was "we, we, we." He repeatedly explained to anyone within earshot that any of the good things going on in the district were the result of the efforts of the great staff in place and their commitment to students, the school district, and the community. Burnley created opportunities to celebrate team collaboration and successes. He consciously worked at every opportunity to reshape this aspect of the organizational culture.

A main outgrowth of the teamwork culture was the concept that all employees facilitate the work of others. Burnley and his top staff worked hard to reshape the bureaucratic paradigm, where bottlenecks and power plays dominated the flow of work. He required every employee, and particularly central office staff, to demonstrate how they were facilitating the work of others. Burnley made it clear to all staff that their job performance and the very existence of their position was predicated on the value of the position to helping others get their work done. This orientation, coupled with a mission driven organization, would go a long way to adding great efficiency and added effectiveness to the school district.

KEYS FOR PERSONAL SURVIVAL

Kenneth Burnley, like all superintendents, is a human being. While humanness might seem, to some, a basic fact that should be accepted at face value, it is all too often completely dismissed or denied when regarding leaders. Leaders are just not expected to display human vulnerability. It is just this reality that makes the successes of a leader such as Ken Burnley so remarkable. While his style allowed him to perform as a tireless, totally focused leader with an exemplary degree of commitment to excellence, the reality of his humanness was, he has admitted, a potential limitation and pitfall. Like other successful leaders, he has learned keys for survival that allow him to continue his pace, focus, and productivity.

The first key for personal survival, according to Burnley, is to invest in your family, creating a safe haven at home. Family and home are the foundation to a successful human being, and when this particular human being is the CEO of a very large organization, the foundation becomes even more critical. Ensuring that family time is sacred, even in the light of multiple demands, is fundamental to stability and a sense of self.

The second key is a personal mandate to keep physically fit. As a lifetime athlete, this superintendent believes that regular physical activity is instrumental in maintaining the health and vitality that are necessary to support a demanding schedule. Furthermore, the accompanying multiple expectations from the school community (both internal and external) and the various stressors that are inherent in this high level position demand the maintenance of a consistently high level of energy.

Third is the maintenance of emotional stability. In such a position, especially within the context of a large school district fraught with such resistance to change and historically status quo culture, criticism and skepticism relative to the superintendent are inevitable. It is essential, says Burnley, not to personalize the criticism. Once personalization begins, confidence, determination, and focus can erode. While the work is often somewhat overwhelming, and positive feedback almost nonexistent, it can be accomplished; therefore, it essential to maintain personal strength.

Fourth, but by no means less important, is the development or perseverance of a spiritual center. One must have a "foundation within" that is based on strong spiritual beliefs, accompanied by ongoing practices designed to maintain a strong core, fortify the soul, provide the requisite courage, increase psychological stamina, and keep the vision in view. Without this key ingredient, says Burnley, nothing else can develop optimally.

RESULTS OF HARD WORK

Leadership, hard work, focus, stability, and intelligence were the key elements that led to the remarkable turnaround of District 11 in Colorado Springs, Colorado. Burnley provided the leadership. He facilitated the work of others and helped them bring their leadership, talent, and hard work to bear on the problems of the district. The results of this leadership have been manifested in many ways, and that story underscores the value of the lessons from this case study of the superintendency.

The effects of this successful leadership have been many, although only a few are highlighted here:

1. Burnley determined that a continuous presence was needed in the state capital to represent the voice of the district (the third largest in the state) relative to the funding formula for public schools. He also convinced board members to hire a lobbyist to work on the district's behalf toward a more appropriate funding allocation from the state. This decision resulted in a shift of classification and, subsequently, a fairer funding base for the district.

2. The district, which continues to grow through increasing enrollment, has improved its position to serve the expanding needs, even though the funding issue statewide continues to be problematic. District 11 opened two new elementary schools in the fall of 1998 with a new middle school opening in fall 1999.

3. The superintendent offered local businesses advertising space on school buses. The suggestion was criticized by internal and external opponents as an exploitation of students. Burnley, however, was not convinced that he should ignore a $1 million addition to the district budget. This controversial innovation not only brought money into district coffers but also strengthened the district's relationship with local business leaders.

4. After years of conflict with a historically active and traditional teachers' union—one that included a community-polarizing teacher's strike in 1975 and a vote of no-confidence in the superintendent in 1990 (primarily due to salary freezes)—district administration now enjoys a new, more collaborative, relationship with union leadership.

5. After years of declining confidence within the community, both internal and external, the district is rebuilding its positive reputation by demonstrating its strengths and publicly acknowledging its efforts to eliminate weaknesses while building a political support base within the community and a more positive relationship with the local media.

6. As a result of the superintendent's leadership and an enhanced relationship with both the teachers' union and the community, the district was successful in passing a $98 million bond election in 1996 after many years of struggle within a community that had historically blocked such actions. The voters in this community had not approved a tax increase since 1972. This bond was passed based on a "guarantee" from the district that student success would follow. If student success were not demonstrated, money would be returned to taxpayers. This success was a tribute to the joint effort between district leadership, the teachers' union, and community leaders.

Leading a school district in such a large and diverse community is always a challenge for superintendents. Looking at districts across the nation reveals a trend toward continuous turnover of superintendents. With each new superintendent comes a time period of stasis before change while the new superintendent studies the district, builds relationships, decides on a plan of action, and begins to move the organization. It is important to acknowledge that part of the foundation for Ken Burnley's success is his ability to maintain the respect of colleagues and community members, and state and national leaders—as well as his choice to remain in this position for eleven years. It is no surprise that he was named National Superintendent of the Year by the American Association of School Administrators in 1993.

RECOMMENDED ACTIVITIES FOR CLASS OR SEMINAR

1. Divide into triads and have each group generate a list of leadership characteristics they believe contributed to the successful outcomes presented in this case study.
2. Independently generate abbreviated case studies of districts facing similar challenges and how superintendents have responded.
3. Analyze the case study and identify competencies that Burnley exhibited that correlate with the AASA Standards for Superintendents (available from the AASA).
4. Evaluate your own competencies, using the AASA Standards for Superintendents and the challenges presented in this case study.</nl>

REFERENCES

Bennis W., and Towsend, R. (1995). *Reinventing Leadership*. New York: Quill.

Bolman, L. G., and Deal, T. D. (1994). *Modern Approaches to Understanding and Managing Organizations*. San Francisco: Jossey-Bass.

Burnley, K. (1997, May). "Staying Afloat." *American School Board Journal*, 32–34.

Carter, G., and Cunningham, W. (1997). *The American School Superintendent*. San Francisco: Jossey-Bass.

Guzmán, N. (1995). "The Leadership Covenant: Essential Factors for Developing Cocreative Relationships within a Learning Community." *Journal of Leadership Studies* 2 (4): 151–160.

Handy, C. (1996). *Beyond Certainty*. Cambridge, MA: Harvard Business School Press.

Jones, R. (1994). "A CEO in the Kid Business." *Executive Educator* 16 (11): 29–31.

Schein, E. H. (1992). *Organizational Culture and Leadership* (2nd ed.). San Francisco: Jossey-Bass.

Warwick, R. (1995). *Beyond Piecemeal Improvements*. Bloomington, IN: National Educational Service.

8

Performance Evaluation:
The Superintendent's Surprise

John R. Hoyle

Dr. E. J. Zatopek is in his third year as superintendent of the South Zulch Independent School District of fifty thousand people. Zatopek had prior administrative experience as a junior high principal and as assistant superintendent for personnel in a large urban district before taking his first superintendency in Rocky Road, a district with twenty-five hundred students in a stable farming community in the western part of the state. He had experienced much success in his first superintendency. His district was cited for high student performance on state and national tests, and over 80% of the graduates attended colleges and universities. The teaching force was stable, and the school board was viewed as supportive of most of Zatopek's programs that he helped develop in his five-year tenure. Also, his football, baseball, and girls basketball teams won district crowns. The South Zulch school board selected Zatopek from a field of fifty-six applicants who met the qualifications for the position. The board was excited to attract a person with a winning track record as their superintendent.

The South Zulch district is within commuting distance to a major midwestern city and has experienced rapid growth in the last ten years. The student population has grown from a little over three thousand to over eight thousand in the past eight years. During that period, the ethnic mix shifted from 95% white students to 62% white, 20% Hispanic, 12% African American, and 6% Asian and Native American.

The students are housed in one high school built in 1961 which has been expanded in a piecemeal fashion to accommodate the enrollment of 2,200, one junior high (grades 8 and 9) that holds 1,100, two middle schools (grades 6 and 7) with over 700 each, two intermediate schools (grades 4 and 5) with over 500 each, six elementary schools (K–3) with an average of 410 each, and an alternative school with an average enrollment of 85. Based on current student enrollment projections, two sites have been identified to build elementary schools in the next three years if the community will support a tax increase. Along with the growth has come an infusion of higher-income professionals from other regions of the nation, Asia, and Europe who commute to the city via the interstate highway. The changing demographics and income levels of the community have created a blend of old rural with the new urban "way of doing things." The composition of the school board has shifted from seven locals who grew up and attended South Zulch schools to three "foreigners" from California, New York, and Michigan and four locals. This board change plus the state department of education's new state accountability requirements have increased the attention and the criticism directed at the schools and school personnel.

The administrators in South Zulch are required by state mandate to display student test scores publicly at each campus and release the campus "report card" to the parents of students at the school and to the local newspaper. A "report card" for each school and for the district is included in a state database system that is readily available on the web. This state accountability system rates each district based on state required test scores, attendance rates, and dropout percentages. The rating categories for the schools are as follows:

1. *Exemplary*, which requires at least 90% of total students and students in African American, Hispanic, White, and Economically Disadvantaged groups to pass the state test in reading, writing, math, science, and social studies, with at least a 94% (grades 1–12) attendance, and 1.0% or lower dropout rate for all students and each student group each semester

2. *Recognized*, which requires at least 80% of total students and students in each group passing each subject tested, a 94.0% (grades 1–12) attendance rate, and a 3.5% or lower dropout rate for all students and each student group

3. *Academically Acceptable*, which requires at least 40% of total students and each student group passing each subject tested, a 94.0% attendance rate (grades 1–12), and above 6.0% or lower dropout rate for all students and each student group

4. *Academically Unacceptable or Low Performing*, which is a result of less than 40.0% of total students and each student group passing each subject tested, less than a 94.0% attendance rate (grades 1–12), and a dropout rate of more than 6.0% for all students or any student group. (The author has adapted the rating categories from the Academic Excellence Indicator System [AEIS], established by the Texas Education Agency, Austin, Texas, 1997.)

These highly visible benchmarks established by the state legislature have increased the pressure on school boards, superintendents, and all staff to excel. Zatopek has felt this increased pressure since the test results for the past year revealed that he had no "exemplary" campuses and only two that were "recognized." Moreover, in the South Zulch High School with more than twenty-two hundred students, only eight were recognized as National Merit Scholars finalists. Seven of these students were recent move-ins, and four of them were of Asian ancestry. The latest scores on the SAT and ACT were not as high as a neighboring district with similar demographics and tax base and were slightly below average for similar districts in the state. The testing landscape was not a pretty picture.

A group of concerned parents who called themselves "Citizens for Quality Schools" had begun meeting in a local church to discuss the "perceived" problems facing the South Zulch schools. The leaders of the group were a husband and wife team who had lived in the district for four years. They had four children in the schools and were very concerned about the quality of education that the children were receiving which was, in their opinion, "not in the same class as the schools we left in Connecticut." The Citizens for Quality Schools group was engaging in talk about school vouchers, private schools, and charter schools and were recruiting other citizens to join their efforts to put, in their words, "pressure on the schools to improve or else."

The Citizens for Quality Schools asked to be included on the next school board agenda to voice their concerns. Zatopek wished that the whole matter would disappear, but he knew that three of his new board members were active "listeners" and friends of the Quality Schools group. He told the group leader that he would be "happy to place them on the next board agenda and looked forward to hearing suggestions to help improve the South Zulch schools." While community leaders were friendly to Zatopek at church and the Rotary Club, he knew that a storm was brewing and it was too late to "batten down the hatches" and ride it out.

Zatopek felt a growing sense of frustration with the performance level of the schools. He had led the board and district personnel in attempting to implement "standards-based" reform, which includes a description of what a student is supposed to know and do (content standards), how well the student is supposed to do it (performance standards), a measure if the student has done it (performance assessment), and a scoring guide to measure each student's performance (rubric). Zatopek really believed that the teaching staff and building principals were on the right track to improve overall student and school performance with the new standards-based education (American Association of School Administrators, 1998).

He increased the budget for staff development for teachers and administrators on topics of school improvement, teaching strategies (i.e., cooperative learning, problem-based learning), and various reading and math programs that had produced results in other districts. He led efforts to disaggregate test data school by school and class by class and brought in consultants on curriculum alignment and at-risk students, but the "high-stakes" test scores still lagged behind. The state department had begun a new statewide teacher and administrator evaluation system that placed more emphasis on each school's performance rather than on the individual teacher or administrator. Even though each teacher and administrator would be evaluated each year, the evaluation would be based on how well the school faculty was working to improve student performance (i.e., test scores, attendance, dropout rate). The primary focus of the new evaluation system was to promote ongoing improvement by using data to improve staff performance through targeted staff development (Walt, 1997). These thoughts on staff improvement flooded Zatopek's mind as he walked to his office to prepare the agenda for the next school board meeting.

The superintendent decided to counteract the Quality Schools group's criticism of the schools and his leadership by presenting his plan for school improvement. He called a meeting of his administrative cabinet and principals to announce a new administrator evaluation system called Administrator Evaluation for Continuous Improvement Model (AECI) (Hoyle, English, & Steffy, 1998; see Figure 8.1). Zatopek told his staff that he and each administrator must begin to shoulder much more responsibility for student performance. "We have spent a lot of time on the standards-based reform system and a lot of money on training you and the teachers on connecting the written, taught, and tested curriculum," he said. "For various reasons we are not making headway fast enough, and the school board and community want to know why."

Zatopek informed them that he had attended a series of seminars conducted by the American Association of School Administrators, which presented the AECI model. He expressed his optimism that the new evaluation model will be the "visionary force" to improve teaching, learning, and state test scores class by class and school by school in the South Zulch district. He explained that the AECI model is a combination of the best thinking from the mutual benefit/goal-setting models, the 360 degree feedback model, and the portfolio process. Zatopek decided to plan a weekend retreat in November that would include members of the board, himself, all administrators, selected teachers and counselors, and community members. He stated that "the model must be based on trust, risk taking, and doing what is best for every child and youth in South Zulch. If we implement the model properly, we should begin to see improvements in student performance in every building in one year's time."

The vision statement for the South Zulch district is "Believing in the worth and dignity of each child and youth by creating rich learning opportunities for life long learning and success." The AECI model would be based on this one-year-old vision, mission, and standards-based goal statements with the support of the board, central office staff, building administrators, site-based teams, and the community. Zatopek then outlined the following steps for implementing the AECI model:

Step 1: The superintendent and a planning committee composed of school board members, administrators (including department heads), and representatives of the district site-based team plan the retreat. In the context of the vision, mission, and goals statements each administrator should write five or six key objectives and a list of activities to be conducted to meet the agreed-on standards in reading, math, writing, science, social studies, and school attendance by the end of the evaluation cycle. In addition, three or four other goals and objectives should be prepared to meet each person's specific job description or role. The opening remarks at the retreat would include the purpose of the process to clarify any misconceptions.

Figure 8.1   Administrator Evaluation for Continuous Improvement Model (AECI)

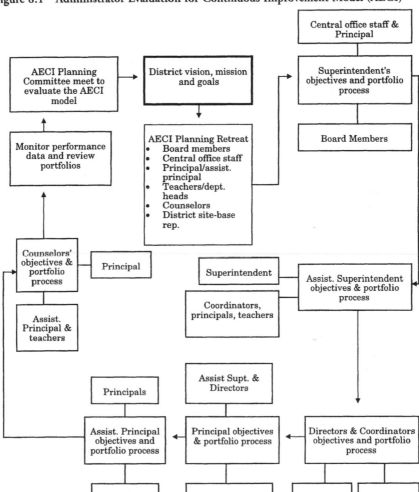

(Reproduction by permission of the American Association of School Administrators, Arlington, VA.)

Step 2: During the first day, all administrators present their goals and objectives to their supervisors and subordinates. The persons most closely affected by the goals will discuss their value in terms of student performance improvement and the methods and processes to be used to reach the student performance standards. Once the goals/objectives and activities are discussed and approved by the small group, members will then discuss methods to monitor each administrator's progress toward accomplishing the goals/objectives to meet the district standards. At this point portfolios will be discussed in terms of their importance in providing supportive evidence of progress toward goal accomplishment (see the model).

Step 3: Zatopek told the group that staff members who report directly to him would discuss their goals/objectives with him and selected others from the district and community. Zatopek would present his goals/objectives to a diverse group who is most directly affected by his leadership (see the model).

Step 4: The retreat will end by insuring the participants that the evaluations will be conducted to help each person improve and lead others to higher performance. Zatopek assured them that everyone will feel comfortable about and will be fully informed about when the evaluations will occur, who will do the evaluating, and what steps will be taken after each evaluation. Each administrator will prepare his/her goals/objectives in triplicate—one copy for the personnel file, one for the key evaluator, and one for the administrator. Also, each administrator will prepare a portfolio as supporting data for the evaluation.

Step 5: Zatopek indicated that a representative from each group at the November retreat should be selected to oversee the AECI process and begin to make plans for the next retreat for January (Hoyle et al., 1998).

Zatopek closed the cabinet and administrator meeting with the following remarks:

> The district and each of us are under attack by a group who feel that we have failed to lead the teachers and students to higher test performance to meet our high standards. Our district and school "report cards," which are based primarily on the state basic skills assessment tests, are not competitive with nearby districts or across the state.
>
> While we have allocated a lot of money and time for staff development on vertical teaming, curriculum and test alignment, and test-taking skills, we have fallen short of the mark. Our critics tend to overlook the increased number of lower socioeconomic and minority students who have moved into the apartment complexes in the district over the last two years, who lower our passing percentages. The critics don't want to hear that we are teaching the "whole child" and not merely teaching to the state test. We will embark on this new administrator evaluation system and let the board know that we are holding ourselves accountable and will work harder to improve test scores for every student over the next two years.
>
> Since the recommended new state evaluation system for teachers has been approved by the legislature and the state board, it is imperative that we set the example for the teachers by beginning this promising AECI model. I can promise you that if the model doesn't work and test scores do not improve, we will be in trouble. Let's make the model work for us to become the best district in this area of the state. Good luck.

THE BOARD MEETING

The following Tuesday evening board meeting was not shaping up to be a positive experience for Zatopek and his staff. The board president, Carol Stern, opened the meeting with the usual rituals, and Zatopek had arranged for the high school chorus to sing *America the Beautiful* for the board and the overflow crowd of teachers, administrators, and over thirty-five members of the Quality Schools group. The special music was well received, and Zatopek hoped that the patriotic music might take some of the edge off of the report by the Quality Schools group.

When the time came on the agenda for the Quality Schools representative to speak, Zatopek felt the pressure building in himself and in the board room. The spokesperson, Dr. Jim Paine, a local dentist, began by saying:

We as the Citizens for Quality Schools express our thanks for the opportunity to appear before the school board and those of you in the audience. We recognize the many accomplishments of this school district and its staff over the years and are here tonight to help make this a better school district for our kids and those who follow. Therefore, on behalf of our Quality Schools group, I make the following observations.

1. We are concerned about the falling test performance by the students in South Zulch. It is very alarming when fewer than 80% of our students fail to pass the state exam that is based on minimal standards for all students in the state. Why are students failing to learn to read, compute basic math, and write simple paragraphs? We have a fairly high tax base comparable to surrounding districts who have higher-rated schools than ours. We should have sixty or seventy National Merit scholars rather than the eight or nine each year. We are concerned about our kids' future success in the universities and in the labor force.

2. We have been concerned about the lack of communication with the schools about our children's progress. Except for the six-week report cards, we know very little about how well our children's performance stacks up with others in the state and nation. We are willing to help the teachers and administrators if we are invited to do so. Keep us informed. Do you want to us to come to your offices and bug you for test and budget information? What are the best universities requiring in terms of SAT and ACT scores and class standing? We need to start our students thinking about the competitive university admissions standards beginning in the sixth grade at least.

3. Also, we are concerned about the caliber of some of our teachers and administrators. We understand that some of the math teachers are not qualified to teach higher math, and the end-of-year algebra test scores are really bad, with only 35% passing. Moreover, researchers tell us that class size should be much smaller than twenty-eight or thirty. Can't we take some of those administrators in the central office and assign them a couple of classes to teach? That would reduce class size and reduce the administrator/teacher ratio overload in the district. Also, we understand that some of the principals and counselors have not been back to school in several years and are not keeping up-to-date on the latest learning technologies, especially the Web and new computer learning packages.

4. Finally, we are concerned about the safety of our kids in the school halls and on

the buses. We have several reports of sexual harassment of our girls by some of the older boys and a lot of bad language in the cafeteria and other places in the buildings. We, as parents, realize that we have an obligation to raise our kids with good manners and respect for authority, but we believe that too much bad behavior is being ignored by school officials and we want you to take measures now to stop it.

We are talking about creating some charter schools and even pulling our kids out and placing them in private schools. We hope that the school board and the administration will take the necessary steps to improve our schools very soon. The superintendent and board are planning to present a multimillion-dollar bond issue to the community next fall. Unless we see the board and staff taking some steps to address the problems we are expressing tonight, we will not support the bond issue. We cannot see pouring good money into a stagnant school system. Thank you for your time and attention.

The board president, Mrs. Carol Stern, thanked Paine for his report and interest in helping the South Zulch district improve. Stern said that Zatopek and his staff will respond as soon as possible about the concerns and that the school board stands ready to help the Quality Schools group with needed information about the schools.

After the Quality Schools crowd left, Stern asked Zatopek to address the board about some of the concerns expressed by Paine. He responded that he would need a couple of days to provide informed responses to the concerns, but that he did want to talk about a new administrator performance model that he wished to implement that would address many of the concerns about student performance. Zatopek presented an overview of the AECI model and asked the board for their support to begin the process immediately. He told the board and the others in the board room that the key to school improvement is the leadership of the principals and those in the central office. He said:

> The buck stops with me and the others in leadership roles. We will write specific performance goals and hold each other accountable for reaching those goals. We believe that our effort to evaluate our performance and hold ourselves accountable for student performance will be a good example for the teaching staff. Within three years our district should be labeled "Recognized," with several of our schools in the "Exemplary" category. I will report my individual goal/objectives to the board after our November retreat. Thank you for your support. We will make you and the people of this community proud of the South Zulch School District.

The November retreat was declared a success. The AECI Planning Committee, consisting of two board members, two central office staff, five principals, three assistant principals, three teachers, one department head from each school campus, three counselors, and eight district site-based team representatives, developed guidelines for the two-day retreat. The retreat was held at a conference center at a nearby lake, and the forty-one participants were transported by a school bus; cellular phones were prohibited to encourage total concentration on the task at hand. Each participant prepared his or her goals/objectives related to the vision and standards/benchmarks. Zatopek and the others presented the procedures on developing action plans, the portfolio process, and a schedule of when the performance of each administrator will be monitored and the individuals who will conduct each appraisal. The process was begun with some fear and trepidation but also with some optimism that the South Zulch children and youth would benefit as a result of the performance evaluation system.

ZATOPEK AND AECI TWENTY MONTHS LATER—DID IT WORK?

Zatopek and each member of the staff followed the AECI steps using data and "best practice" strategies to improve personal, staff, and student performance. The second November retreat went very smoothly, and student test and attendance rates were moving in the right direction. One elementary school reached "Exemplary," status and three more schools became "Recognized," with two others barely missing the mark. One middle school principal was encouraged to retire early since her school remained "Low Performing." Four other principals were placed on "performance probation" by Zatopek; and seven principals, twelve assistant principals, and two counselors were required to attend workshops on curriculum alignment and strategies to help "front-load" the curriculum to match the state test items. Zatopek decided that he, his director of curriculum, and five content specialists should attend three state department training seminars on test alignment and technology.

These professional development steps were taken with the hope that major improvements in student performance would become evident after the second year. The state test scores, SAT, ACT, and other standardized test scores were bound to be much better after all of the hard work by the administrative staff over the last twenty months. After all, Zatopek's favorite quote is "Remember, leaders have to set the tone for excellence. You can't light a fire with a wet match." He knew that the new test results were to be made available to the district in the next ten days. Zatopek asked a friend, John Apple, in the state department school accountability office to allow him to see the test results before anyone else in the district. After all, Zatopek said to his friend, "I want to contact Mrs. Stern and Dr. Paine, staff, and the community and tell them the good news."

THE RESULTS

Zatopek returned to his office at 8:01 A.M. on Monday morning, two weeks since his talk with John Apple at the state department of education. He noticed a fax on his desk from the state department division of school accountability. He had a lump in his throat as he turned the pages that held the fate of his district and maybe his professional future. His eyes were riveted to the scores for the high school, middle, and elementary campuses. The high school dropped from "Recognized" to "Acceptable" because two Hispanics had dropped out and the attendance rate was only 93%. The test scores were up in math, reading, and remained the same in writing, science, and social studies. His heart sank as he continued to review his district data. The same elementary school was rated "Exemplary," two middle schools and three elementary schools were "Recognized," and no school dropped into the "Low Performing" category. However, the South Zulch district did not reach Zatopek's goal of being "Recognized."

To add insult to injury, Zatopek received his annual performance evaluation as part of the annual AECI process. It was less than a pretty picture. While his board members gave him high to average ratings on his job as superintendent and on his performance levels on each of his written goals/objectives, his subordinates in the central office and district principals and selected teachers were less positive in their evaluations. He had high ratings on his efforts to build a shared vision for student success and in keeping the board and the community informed about student performance. His ratings in providing targeted staff development and follow-up on the training for teachers and administrators were average, but his appraisal scores on his effort to provide each school the necessary central office support to improve the teaching and learning environment to move each school to "Recognized" status was given an unsatisfactory rating.

As he reviewed his evaluation, Zatopek took a deep breath as he felt his blood pressure and heart rate rocket upward. The following thoughts and questions ricocheted in his mind: Why had he failed the district? Why didn't all of his hard work and leadership pay off in higher student performance? He had promised the board, community, staff, and students that in three years the district would be "Recognized" with several "Exemplary" schools. What went wrong? Was the AECI model the wrong choice? What do I do now? Should I resign before the board decides to not renew my contract beyond the next two years? Zatopek called his wife to tell her the bad news. This was not going to be a nice day for him. He began thinking what he would tell his board the next afternoon in a closed session to discuss the test scores and his evaluation.

RATIONALE FOR APPLYING PERFORMANCE EVALUATION TO ATTACK THE PROBLEM

Next to low test scores and public criticism, performance evaluation is perhaps the most perplexing problem in education. After many years of experimenting with various strategies to evaluate the performance of people on the job, the search for solutions to the problem and a perfect model continues. The most puzzling problem for educational leaders is finding the link between administrator behavior and student performance on tests of all kinds. Ronald Berk (1986) defines performance assessment this way: "Performance assessment is the process of gathering data by systematic observation for making decisions about an individual" (p. ix). Berk suggests four key elements in this definition. First, assessment is a process. Second, the focus is on data gathering. Third, systematic data gathering is stressed. Fourth, the data are integrated for the purpose of making specific decisions. The AECI model is a framework that includes these four elements. How does an evaluator incorporate the rational (objective) and constructivist (process) components into a performance evaluation and make it valid, fair, and a vehicle for continuous improvement for the individual and the school or district? Was Zatopek treated fairly and in a professional manner? How much misery did the superintendent heap on himself? While the performance evaluation and student achievement problem may differ with the size of the school district, it is not unique. The solutions to solving the mysteries between administrator performance and district student performance must be found before the lives of superintendents can keep a proper balance between "butterflies and ulcers."

LEARNING ACTIVITIES

1. Divide the class or workshop participants into groups of six to eight persons. If the graduate class or seminar group is small (i.e., eight to ten), keep them in one group. Either appoint a discussion leader or ask the group/s to pick the person with the most recent birthday to be the discussion leader.
2. Ask each person to read and take notes on the case and be prepared to discuss the following questions:
   a. What do we know about the South Zulch school district?
   b. How has the school board composition changed in recent years?
   c. What do we know about Zatopek as a professional educator?
   d. Would you use the same approach to improve student performance that Zatopek used?
   e. What are the key components of the AECI evaluation model?
   f. How would you use the AECI model to improve the South Zulch schools?
   g. What would you prepare to say to the board next Monday afternoon?
   h. Select a theory (e.g., leadership, motivation, goal theory, interpersonal sensitivity, or human factors) to help frame and solve the problem.

ROLE PLAY

Appoint group members to play the roles of E. J. Zatopek; Mrs. Carol Stern, board president; and Dr. Jim Paine, spokesperson for the Citizens for Quality Schools. The setting is a closed meeting with the board to offer Zatopek a chance to respond to the suggestions and criticisms Paine presented at the recent board meeting. Zatopek is nervous, Stern is being "political" in her remarks, and Paine is his "total expert" and community self-appointed hero self. Stern opens the meeting and introduces Paine, who is invited to make any remarks as points of clarification before calling on Zatopek to make his report. The others in the group will play the role of other board members—three foreigners and three locals (Carol Stern is a local). Set a time limit of forty minutes—and go for it!

REFERENCES

American Association of School Administrators. (August, 1998). *When Standards Drive Change*. Arlington, VA: Panasonic Foundation in collaboration with the American Association of School Administrators.

Berk, R. (1986). *Performance Assessment*. Baltimore, MD: Johns Hopkins University Press.

Hoyle, J., English, F., and Steffy, B. (1998). *Skills for Successful Twenty-first Century School Leaders*. Arlington, VA: American Association of School Administrators.

Texas Education Agency. (1997). "TAAS Scores to Help Grade the Teachers." *Houston Chronicle*, 5A.

Walt, K. (1997, January 30). *Accountability Manual*. Austin: Office of Policy Planning and Research, Texas Education Agency.

9

When Restructuring a School Includes Transforming a Principal's Leadership

Patsy E. Johnson and Cheryl Holder

PRIMARY FOCUS

This case centers around solving leadership and teaching problems through school restructuring.

KEY ISSUES

- New superintendent
- Conflict and hostility within school faculty
- Teacher and parent complaints concerning school and principal
- School board pressure
- Political implications for dismissing a principal
- Teacher empowerment
- School restructuring
- Changing the school culture

KEY LEARNING OBJECTIVES

- To describe effective dimensions of leadership utilized to solve problems of school leadership, student underachievement, faculty conflict, and community politics
- To analyze the leadership issues creating the problem
- To identify alternative responses to the problem and their consequences
- To assess the selected strategy

117

THE CASE

During the past decade, educators across North America have been experimenting with restructuring schools and school systems. One effort has been directed toward changing the way issues are considered and decisions are made in individual schools. The dominant concept has been some form of shared decision making in which autocratic control of the superintendent and principal gives way to meaningful participation of teachers—and in some instances parents—in the governance structure of the school. Although many school systems are under some mandate to implement the concept of site-based management and shared decision making, some school systems are voluntarily adopting one or more of its features.

Such moves to a shared governance model in education are typically made as a means to improve student performance. This goal rests on the rationale that teachers, who are directly involved in the classroom, are in the best position to make decisions regarding their teaching. Underlying this reasoning is the notion that a single central leader does not or cannot always make the best educational decisions without significant input from a diverse group of stakeholders in the outcomes of decisions. A second underlying reality is that where moves to shared decision making are considered, some dissatisfaction had been experienced with an existing hierarchical and autocratic system. In some instances, this dissatisfaction had escalated into intense and dysfunctional conflict. Shared decision making was seen as a possible means to reduce the conflict and improve the educational product.

The move to shared decision making contains the risk that the replacement governance structure is no more or even less effective than its precursor. It is not uncommon for teachers, when faced with the prospect of becoming more involved in the decision-making process, to respond that they do not have the time or interest to participate in the school governance. They will also complain that they do not have the necessary expertise and training to make informed judgments about the many issues that face the school's leader. They will observe that they are not paid to assume the responsibilities of school leadership. Such negative responses often surface when other teachers are eager to become involved in decision making. These teachers see this new opportunity as the one real chance to make changes that are long overdue. They see that their expertise in facilitating student learning could be utilized to make schoolwide decisions that would have a positive impact on student performance. When such divisions are found in the faculty, the move to shared governance rests on a bed of conflict.

A second source of conflict is the school leader. In those circumstances where the school leader perceives a loss of power or the ability to make decisions on issues over which he or she will be held accountable, the tendency is to resist the move. The principal can sabotage the change process through subtle or overt means. Meetings can be delayed, announcements never made, severe time demands on the faculty predicted, and threats making life difficult for the faculty offered. Some principals welcome shared decision making, but for the wrong reason. They see it as an opportunity to abdicate their leadership responsibilities by deferring all difficult and unpopular decisions to the decision-making body—school council, parent-faculty committee, and so forth.

Understanding the dynamics associated with a change in governance structure of a school requires the careful analysis of such factors as the history of the school, the personalities of the players in the scenario, the sociopolitical climate of the community, and the power and policy dynamics surrounding the superintendent and the school board. This analysis will reveal a combination of features that is unique to each situation. Even though there is a unique set of features for each case, many of the underlying issues are found as threads that run through most school organizations. Therefore, the examination of one case should be relevant to the consideration of the broader issues that are common to a variety of school settings. This examination can be facilitated by using Bolman and Deal's (1997) four frames of analysis. These are the political, structural, human resources, and symbolic frames.

Overview

The case is presented as a chronology of events that occurred before, during, and after a governance restructuring effort at Lincoln Grammar School. The project in terms of planning, intervention, and maintenance occurred over a three-year period as part of a larger restructuring effort in Consolidated School District 67. The direction and expertise of an outside consultant guided the project. Data for the case were gathered from surveys, formal and informal interviews, transcripts and minutes of meetings, and documents produced by the teachers and principal of the elementary school and the superintendent of the district. Names, dates, and some details of the case have been changed to honor assurances of confidentiality and to protect the identity of the community and individuals involved. The narrative begins with a description of background events and situations from which grew the problem and the rationale to change the governance structure of the school. The narrative continues with a description of how the problem was addressed by the superintendent. The next section describes how the new governance model was implemented over a three-year period. The principal's reactions to the process are described next, which are followed by a description of the processes used in the evaluation of the project. The narrative concludes with a discussion of the case from the perspective of the four frames of analysis (Bolman & Deal, 1997).

Past Leadership

Randall Blackburn had been hired one year ago as the new superintendent of Consolidated School District 67. He was following the leadership of Howard Stone, the previous superintendent of this small city school system of approximately four thousand students, which for the ten years of his office had been typical of many such school districts in the region. Authority was centralized; decision making resided mainly in the superintendents' and principals' offices. Nationwide trends to adopt school-based decision making and teacher empowerment had been ignored. Stone's governance style had been dogmatic. Administrative decisions from the district office had been micromanaged and tightly controlled, leaving little room for input from principals and teachers. Similar governance styles had been adopted by individual principals in the school district.

Most of the teachers and principals had long associations with CSD 67. They remembered the administration of Stone's predecessor whose governance style was close to laissez-faire. Having witnessed conflict escalate in that setting to such a point that the teachers staged a strike, parents and teachers were, at first, appreciative of Stone's "no-nonsense" policy. The school board had also supported Stone's actions, having cited them as the way to refocus the district on the education of students. However, after several years, this autocratic style had begun to wear thin. Complaints from district personnel and community members were heard about stifling regulations and dictatorial rule. Stone had developed a confrontational style and was aggressively carrying his agenda to the school board with an adversarial tone. Sensing the growing discontentment among parents and teachers, Stone left for another school system that "appreciated his leadership abilities."

The school board then conducted a national search and selected Blackburn. Among his first leadership steps were efforts to address the high levels of conflict found within the faculties of most of the schools and the relatively low levels of student academic performance revealed by national and state standardized achievement tests.

The New Leadership Style

The principals in each school had heard the term *site-based management* during Blackburn's interviews. They knew that the autocratic, confrontational style of the previous administration was to be challenged by the new superintendent, but that understanding gave them little insight into how the new leader's beliefs would translate into changes in their own leadership behavior. They did observe that Blackburn's meetings with the principals became more collaborative and consultative than in their previous experience. However, the principals did not apply this model to their own administrative units. Therefore, governance continued in individual buildings much as it had under the previous administration. Blackburn discovered that each school had similar needs to be addressed: resolving conflicts within the faculty and between the faculty and the principal, motivating teachers to make changes and to try new instructional approaches, improving communications with parents, and energizing the instructional climate.

The School in Trouble

Blackburn believed that one school in CSD 67, Lincoln Grammar, had reached a point of crisis. The amount of conflict was high, motivation of teachers was low, communication with parents concerning student learning issues was minimal, and the educational climate was, at best, flat. Some teachers were creating public relations problems for the school by venting their frustrations to parents and other community members. Other teachers, especially new ones, found themselves in a hostile teaching environment. New ideas and approaches that were brought in by the newcomers were rejected by the old guard as ineffective, out of touch with reality and passing educational fads.

However, these circumstances had resulted not from an autocratic style of Buddy Morris, the principal, but from the abdication of his leader power and responsibilities. Finding the autocratic style of the previous administration difficult to manage, the principal yielded his authority to an influential core group of teachers. This unofficial base of power had become so dominating within the school governance structure that the principal typically avoided making decisions that would upset the status quo. These teachers were able to intimidate other teachers and the principal with their collective belligerence toward any suggestion of change. They also adopted a very rigid code for student discipline and made life difficult for any teacher who did not support it.

The resulting conflicts between teachers and parents were exacerbated with a very combative style of communication from the teachers. Any sense of collegiality within the faculty was nonexistent. Name calling, cursing, and other forms of belligerence between teachers were common. No collective effort existed for the solution of schoolwide problems or problems for a specific grade level. Teachers became isolated in their own classrooms and worked to their own ends and purposes. Any real or perceived transgression of another teacher's sovereignty or rights was met with aggressive hostility. Central office personnel were frequently called to the school to resolve conflicts within the faculty and between the faculty, the principal, and the parents. Although the group of teachers constituting the power core was generally satisfied with the state of affairs, other teachers found the school to be a horrible place to work.

The Crisis Event

Blackburn decided to intervene in the Lincoln Grammar's governance after two parents contacted the local television station to complain about a teacher's inflexibility in dealing with their children with attention deficit/hyperactivity disorder (ADHD). This publicity exposed many of the school's problems to the entire community. Buddy Morris discounted the reports of conflict and inflexibility within his school and claimed that students' scores on standardized tests were sufficiently high to suggest that the school was "doing things right." The superintendent realized that such denials would not be well received by the school board and the community.

Blackburn began his intervention by asking several questions: Should central office personnel be sent to the school to help the principal fulfill his leadership role? Should Morris be terminated and replaced with a more effective leader? Should outside expertise be tapped to help implement systemic changes in school governance that would lead to an improved school climate and reduced conflict?

The Principal

Answering these questions was difficult because of the interpersonal relationships established by Morris with many parents of students at Lincoln Grammar. First, he had created an image of caring about the children in the school. During his long tenure at the school, he had developed many ties with the community through religious and service-related associations projecting the image that he was a school leader that could be trusted. He was quick to engage parents in polite pleasantries expressing an interest in their children and other family concerns. He appeared sympathetic to any parental complaint involving one or more of the teachers, and he tended to pass blame to someone else or to circumstances beyond his control for problems found at the school. Even though the teachers expressed privately that they believed Morris to be an ineffective leader, they never called for his ouster, because they liked him. He devoted considerable energy to projecting a caring image by telephoning when a teacher or a teacher's family member was ill. A death in a family brought an immediate response of food delivered to the grieving family's home. Such personal touches were noted and appreciated. Any attempt to dismiss this principal likely would have been met with considerable resistance from teachers and parents and might have placed the new superintendent's job in jeopardy.

ADDRESSING THE PROBLEM

Setting a Goal

Superintendent Blackburn decided on an approach that was designed to effect systemic changes in the school without Principal Morris appearing threatened. Blackburn recognized that changes in the established power structure would take time and skillful application of organizational change strategies. He broached the subject of needed changes in the school by revealing to Morris his commitment to expand the number of participants in decision making at all educational levels in the school system. Blackburn wanted to conduct a pilot project with shared decision making in Lincoln Grammar School that would serve as a model for the remaining schools in the district. The objective would be to develop a climate of respect and teamwork among the faculty, administration, students, and parents within a frame of shared decision making. A consultant in educational leadership from a university in the area would be engaged to develop a change plan and conduct a long-term staff development project. (The consultant had been meeting with Blackburn and had already suggested the direction the superintendent should take when dealing with the problem school.)

The consultant began planning with Blackburn and a central office staff supervisor. Two purposes were agreed on: to develop an organizational structure that would allow for a more equitable shared governance between the teachers and the principal, and to assist the principal in developing a more productive leadership style that incorporates team building and conflict management strategies. It was estimated that significant progress in realizing these purposes would take at least three years.

Shaping Attitudes

The first phase of the project was shaping attitudes regarding issues of school governance. The purpose was to involve the faculty, principal, superintendent, and consultant in a candid discussion of issues facing the school. Faculty members were also asked for opinions regarding how a change in the school's governance might help address those issues. The term *site-based management* was used to refer to the proposed school governance-restructuring concept. Initial teacher reactions to suggestions that they become more involved in a collaborative leadership process ranged from enthusiasm for the opportunity to make substantive changes in operations of the school to dismissive disinterest in an activity that "teachers were not hired to do." However, the consultant urged all participants to consider the benefits of a shared decision-making culture. Strongly encouraged by Blackburn, Morris stated his commitment to participate fully in any plan that was developed. Blackburn revealed to Lincoln Grammar's faculty his resolve to move the school district in the direction of the school-based decision-making model. These shows of support for the project helped to forge a consensus among the faculty to begin working on the change in school governance at Lincoln Grammar. The significance of the faculty members' participation was heightened by their understanding that this change in governance was a pilot project for the school system.

Gathering Baseline Data

Data regarding the amount of organizational conflict experienced by the teachers were gathered with a conflict survey instrument. The results of this survey indicated overall high levels of interpersonal conflict. Individual interviews were also conducted with all teachers and staff members. Each person was asked to respond to questions regarding teacher empowerment, organizational conflict, and the instructional climate at the school. Analysis of these data revealed that the faculty members tended to experience high amounts of conflict because of hostile feelings and distrust toward one another. Conflicts that they experienced with Morris tended to be rooted in his failure to deal with problems in the school that were important to the teachers. These ranged from dirty classrooms and restrooms to having only one telephone line to serve the entire school. Faculty members' questions regarding implementation of decisions, such as "What ever happened to the maintenance work on the floors that we decided was a top priority?" were either ignored or passed off with "I'm still working on that."

The data analysis strengthened Blackburn's resolve to implement shared decision-making as an effective alternative to the existing situation. His reasoning was that if participants were part of the decision-making process, they would feel ownership in the process and would devote more attention to following through with planned initiatives. The teachers would stop identifying the principal's inaction as the source of their conflict because the decision-making and oversight responsibility would have been shifted, in part, to the faculty.

Making a Commitment

Blackburn's understanding of change theory and processes led him to realize that, at first, the amount of conflict could increase when planned changes were implemented. With this in mind, he recommended that sufficient time and training be devoted to altering the leadership and governance culture of the school. The consultant began a three-year commitment to the project involving extensive and ongoing staff development. The aim was to secure a culture of teamwork among the faculty and to retool the leadership skills of the principal. Blackburn maintained high visibility in the process by injecting himself periodically into the process to attend faculty meetings wherein he would reaffirm his commitment to the project, respond to questions, and comment on progress or problems. In addition, Blackburn met regularly with Morris regarding details of the project and applied pressure on the principal to accept the recommendations of the consultant and the decisions of the faculty on specific governance and operational issues. His encounters with Morris often utilized feedback from the faculty and suggestions obtained from the consultant.

Adopting Project Metaphors

Team performance and collaboration were the metaphors that served to identify the operational philosophy of the new governance plan. The teachers realized team performance meant that people within working groups must shed some of their individuality and accept some goals and purposes that are products of the group. Implied in this realization is that individual group members must trust the collective wisdom emerging from team action and that each person should view the actions and motives of others in the group as valuable and nonthreatening. The faculty began its introduction to the team performance concept with a series of activities that were designed to answer four questions: Why am I here? Who are we? What are we doing? How do we do it? Integrated into the question-answer process were discussions about conflicts over values and beliefs and from the perceptions of gains or losses of resources, power, influence, and other issues of self-interest.

The faculty and administration adopted a series of statements that served to articulate the rationale and expectations for the shared decision-making model. They included the following:

1. Through the process of consensus building, a clear, focused common mission and vision will be sought and articulated by participants (including staff, students, parents, and community).
2. Participants will develop an ownership of the plan and therefore a commitment to carry out the goals and activities.
3. Through the efforts of committed and focused participants, the school will successfully achieve the goals and activities selected to implement the plan.
4. The success of the plan will positively impact student learning.

The following mission statement was adopted: "We will become a team committed to the group, as well as to the individuals within the group, for the betterment of education at our school." Adoption of these guidelines led to the next step, the development of action plans.

Creating Action Plans

Through consultant-led discussion and small-group brainstorming, a series of decision-making areas emerged. They were Student Behavior, Student Services, School Climate, Staff Development, Resources and Technology, and Curriculum. The faculty agreed that an effective way to address these issues was to form a series of action teams to address each of the decision-making areas. Each team was charged with the responsibility of studying the concerns relevant to its area facing the school and planning appropriate measures for dealing with those concerns. After answering the questions "What are we doing?" and "How do we do it?" each team began developing its own action plan by asking the questions "Who does what, when, and where?" Each faculty member was asked to serve on only one team of her choosing. Participation was 100%.

The action teams reported their recommendations to the entire faculty at regularly scheduled schoolwide faculty meetings. The entire faculty had the opportunity to participate in considering any recommendation from an action team; thus, any decision represented the will of the entire faculty, not merely the group of teachers on an individual action team. This process improved communication throughout the school and garnered support and commitment from the entire faculty for recommendations that were adopted.

IMPLEMENTING THE NEW GOVERNANCE MODEL

First Year

The first year of the project focused on team building, conflict management, decision making by consensus, conducting meetings, and planning. The initial tasks were to define the functions of the teams, develop a mission and purpose, identify roles and responsibilities, and articulate goals and activities. During the first year, each team addressed its list of issues and assigned priorities based on its perceived needs and its ability to proceed with an effective agenda. As action teams assumed areas of responsibility, duplicated effort from a preexisting uncoordinated ad hoc committee structure was reduced or eliminated. The teams also identified other issues related to their mission and purpose and added them to their responsibilities. As the work of the faculty progressed, the need for two additional action teams was recognized—the Support Staff Action Team and the Parents Action Team. The Support Staff Action Team consisted of secretarial, custodial, and food service personnel. The Parents Action Team was open to any parent wanting to attend. Both teams served as focus interview groups to tap ideas and brainstorm issues representing perspectives of individuals who were not professional educators. They were also challenged to offer action strategies appropriate for their constituencies that would help improve student learning at Lincoln Grammar School.

The schedule of faculty meetings provided regular meeting times for each action team and general faculty interaction. Aides and other support personnel were included in these meetings. Also, the schedule was intended to assure that the shared decision-making planning process was not added to an already crowded meeting schedule. Action teams, grade-level meetings, and general faculty meetings were held on one designated Monday per month after regular school hours. Special meetings were arranged on nonassigned Mondays.

Second Year

During the second year, the action team plans begun in the first year were continued as well as occasional reviews of the topics of the first year (team building, conflict management, etc.). Block scheduling was installed to provide time for teacher collaboration and planning. The daily schedule divided the school day into three instructional blocks. All of the "pull-out" programs (e.g., music, art, library, counseling classes, Indian education, Chapter I, and special education) were scheduled during one block. Consequently, the other two blocks had minimal fragmentation and disruption. Also, planning was emphasized with a formal guide for the process. This planning was directed to what each action team could do to improve student learning. The planning process addressed the following considerations: problem statement, causes, goals, assessment target, activities, resources required, people and their skills and knowledge, materials, time, funds, and indicators of attainment.

Third Year

In the third year, the plans were continued and implemented with ongoing revision and adjustment. Also, the action teams were reconfigured to include a balance of members across grade levels.

RESPONSES OF THE PRINCIPAL

Buddy Morris was faced with having to make some major adjustments in his long-established routines for conducting his office. He had been content to allow the school to exist without a direction, vision, or clear purpose. He had become the master of putting things off. He would try to disengage quickly in a conflict scenario, hoping that if he could avoid the problem long enough it would go away, or at least die down. Through his avoiding and procrastinating behavior, he was able to soften demands of his job to the point that he could close his office door and take a break to watch commercial television programs on a TV set that he had installed in his office.

Superintendent Blackburn had upset his system. An outside consultant was intruding in Morris's building regularly, talking to teachers, staff members, parents, and him, and taking significant chunks of time during faculty meetings. A central office administrator also kept tabs on the project. Teachers were being organized and assigned tasks. The principal was under pressure from these intrusions into his comfortable domain to make some changes that he neither wanted to make nor believed should be made. However, his cooperation was necessary because Blackburn made it clear to him that he was responsible for coordinating and seeing to it that planned actions and activities were carried out. But Morris believed that he had too many other responsibilities for running the school that were more pressing than these governance changes. Because of this, he began his interaction with the project by ignoring requests of the consultant to set up times for teachers to meet in small groups to begin the work of the action teams. In some ways, his intransigence was bolstered when some of the faculty members came to him to complain that they did not really want to make decisions for running the school. "That was *his* job."

The consultant had organized the faculty to work in action teams during one of the visits to the school and fully expected the faculty to have the opportunity to begin developing their action plans. On the next visit, the consultant found that Morris had not bothered to organize a meeting schedule for these action teams. Instead, he had called faculty meetings to pursue his own agenda with no mention of the action teams.

Blackburn summoned Morris to the central office for a private conference. He asked Morris for a status report of the "pilot" project for the school system, indicating that he wanted Morris to give him a monthly status report on the work of each action team. Blackburn assured the principal that he had a lot of confidence in the principal's ability to provide the necessary leadership to make the project a success. Blackburn's tone and the way he emphasized his backing of the project made Morris aware that his future as the leader of the Lincoln Grammar School depended on his full cooperation and involvement in the restructuring process.

This nudge by Blackburn had a profound effect on Morris's actions. Morris seemed to realize that the orders were coming from Blackburn, not from the consultant. He was too young to retire, and he was too weak in his position to resist any more. The message had become clear: cooperate and become a leader in the project or lose the position as principal.

This hands-on approach by Blackburn was the spark that was needed to get the project moving. After his conference with Blackburn, Morris devised a new plan for meetings of the action teams. The meetings were scheduled, and each action team began its work. A month later, a faculty meeting was called for each team to give its first report for discussion and feedback. The superintendent was invited to attend this meeting. It was clear to the faculty that Blackburn was serious about shared governance and was counting on the teachers to make it work. Morris and Blackburn answered questions regarding policy, budgets, and school law. With this meeting, the teachers began to see that they could make decisions regarding the operation of the school that would be acted upon by the principal and superintendent. The meeting also provided a sense that their decision-making powers were limited because ultimate approval of all decisions resided with the superintendent and the school board.

EVALUATION

As the project progressed, data were gathered regarding teachers' self-perceptions about intrapersonal and interpersonal dimensions that had a potential impact on the outcome of implementing the shared governance concept. In addition to adding to the data regarding the amount of conflict obtained for baseline purposes at the beginning of the study, instruments were administered to the faculty regarding teacher empowerment and the power bases of the principal. It was reasoned that if the decision-making processes and its outcomes were more to the liking of the faculty and principal, teachers would feel more empowered, the personal power bases of the principal would become stronger and the position power bases would become weaker, and the amount of conflict within self, with peers, and with the principal would decrease.

Five data collection points were utilized over the three-year span of the project, including the initial pretest for intra- and interpersonal conflict. Conflict amounts generally declined over the span of the project. Teacher empowerment also increased steadily during the same time. Measures of the five bases of leader power also revealed shifts during the course of the study. Scores for referent, expert, and legitimate power increased, while scores for coercing power declined somewhat. Reward power remained relatively low.

CASE ANALYSIS

Superintendent Blackburn was faced with an organization that was significantly dysfunctional. The principal at Lincoln Grammar School made decisions that were not aligned with best practice in educational leadership, he was not meeting the expectations of what the community needed and wanted for the education of the students, and he was not meeting the professional needs of the faculty and staff. Perhaps his behavior could be explained as a response to the intimidation he must have felt under the dominating and dictatorial style of the previous superintendent. He avoided taking actions when he feared that he would be criticized for poor decision making. The superintendent was expected to take appropriate action to correct this intolerable situation. His actions can be considered within the context of the four theoretical frames described by Bolman and Deal (1997).

Structural Frame

The first frame to consider is structural. The basic understanding regarding structure is that educating children is a complex task and that simple organizational structures are not adequate for the challenges. The single boss over a cadre of subordinates with top-down communication will likely yield disappointing results. Although this was the official organizational structure at Lincoln Grammar School, the reality was that the principal had abdicated his decision-making role to inaction, procrastination, avoidance, and laziness. Teachers had filled the void in the leadership structure through a type of "adhocracy" (Bolman & Deal, p. 68) in which a core group of teachers become the locus of control and authority. This arrangement was ineffective because the core group was absorbed in preserving its own self-interests and was unable to consider issues beyond their limited perspective. The superintendent countered these conditions with a plan to implement a new structure in which small teams were organized that crossed the established ad hoc divisions within the faculty and dispersed the power throughout the faculty. A provision was made for intercommunication between teams and the principal with a new understanding that the superintendent expected the new structure to yield decisions that would be implemented.

Human Resources Frame

Closely related to the structural frame were issues involving individuals that made up the organization. These issues fall under the human resources frame. These people had beliefs, attitudes, feelings, needs, and desires that affected their behaviors and, hence, the behavior of the organization. The superintendent found that a simple removal of the principal would be difficult because of the interpersonal relationships that had emerged over many years. The faculty wanted something to be done about the incompetence of the principal, but they also did not want him to get hurt. These warm feelings toward the principal were also found in the community. The superintendent could not overlook the potential disruption to the education process and the potential risk to his own position by ignoring these potent human resources dimensions.

Political Frame

Another set of interpersonal dimensions is best understood within the political frame. Individual and group interests interweave to form a dynamic complex of interactions and reaction. Within this orientation, like-minded individuals will form coalitions to achieve some objective or maintain a position. Often, such coalitions form as a result of some kind of conflict. These two characteristics, coalitions and conflict, were characterizing features of Lincoln Grammar School. The superintendent recognized that the coalition of teachers for the status quo, the older group, had the upper hand because of entrenchment in the community, confidence in "being right," and greater experience in manipulating the system. The much looser coalition of younger teachers had their ideas easily beaten down with ridicule, sarcasm, and dismissive indifference. His approach was to alter the usual organizational political balance with the introduction of an outside consultant who, with expertise and experience not easily countered by the old guard, reorganized the faculty so that the established coalitions were weakened to the point of having minimal impact on the new organizational initiatives.

Symbolic Frame

The symbolic frame embraces the notion that people are defined as who they are. The superintendent encountered a principal who had defined himself as a caring, helpful, and thoughtful person who was interested in helping people in their times of need. He was the good shepherd of his flock. Although this metaphor had nothing to do with the principal's leadership, it had everything to do with his staying power. The superintendent looked on this pastoral image as the principal's one asset, an asset that had considerable power and influence within the faculty and community. Removing the principal because of incompetence would have been resisted because of his perceived redeeming values that had been developed over many years. The new superintendent's negative judgments would have been suspect by a constituency who tended to believe any problems the principal had were beyond his control. Decency and compassion formed his image; decency and compassion were valued as important qualities in the leadership of the school.

OUTCOMES

- Superintendent seen as effective problem solver
- Improved principal performance
- Reduced faculty conflict
- Hostile energy redirected to creative energy
- Reduction in complaints by faculty
- Faculty now seen as collaborative and working together

UNIQUE ASPECTS OF THE CASE

- Leadership role abdicated by principal
- No room for dismissal or transfer of the principal
- Support for principal from parents and teachers in spite of apparent incompetence
- Destructive response of principal to teacher negativism

DISCUSSION QUESTIONS

1. Assuming the superintendent's fears of an adverse reaction to firing the principal were unfounded, what course of action would have been appropriate to take?
2. What alternatives might the superintendent have considered instead of:
   a. bringing in an outside consultant?
   b. restructuring the governance to include shared decision making?
   c. injecting himself directly into the change process?
   d. employing team-building strategies to reorganize the faculty?
   e. pressuring the principal to actively support the governance changes and the staff development plan?
3. Which of the problems identified at Lincoln Grammar School seem most serious?
4. What resources might have been used by the consultant and superintendent to develop an approach to solving the problems at Lincoln Grammar School?
5. What is the likelihood that the governance at Lincoln Grammar School will return to its original state following the completion of the three-year project?
6. What steps should the superintendent take to assure that the faculty and administration at Lincoln Grammar continue to work for the improvement of the school through collaborative decision making?
7. What additional improvements might the superintendent expect the principal and the faculty to make after completing the three-year project?
8. Are three years sufficient to make systemic changes in the school's governance structure?
9. What are the moral, ethical, and legal issues facing the superintendent?
10. Is the superintendent putting the children's education at Lincoln Grammar School on hold while he tries his three-year experiment?
11. What report might the superintendent make to the school board after the three-year project that would justify his actions? Consider this report from two frames: (a) the school board is friendly and supportive, and (b) the school board is hostile and critical.
12. What are the potential public relations implications for the superintendent if the project were perceived as a failure?

REFERENCES

Bolman, L. G., and Deal, T. E. (1997*). Reframing Organizations: Artistry, Choice, and Leadership* (2nd ed.). San Francisco: Jossey-Bass.

10

Examining a Superintendent's Instructional Leadership: Translating Beliefs into Actions

John L. Keedy and Ann G. Mullin

ADMINISTRATIVE PROBLEM AND CASE OBJECTIVES

Fifteen years ago Cuban (1984) predicted that the pressure for school change would transform the role of the superintendent from manager to curriculum expert. In the 1990s, school reformers complemented this curriculum role of the superintendent with the need for central office personnel to support school-level improvement efforts. Significant education change is possible only with "coordinated co-development of schools and districts" (Fullan, 1993, p. 147). Change and improvement is a two-way street. Districts must support the improvement efforts of schools through goal clarification, resources, and political support (Keedy & Allen, 1998; Louis & Miles, 1990); principals and teachers need the autonomy to make decisions on behalf of their clientele, the students.

Unfortunately, superintendents, according to several researchers, have not become district leaders for supporting school-site instructional improvement. Crowson and Morris (1991, p. 210) found that superintendents still operated at the institutional level at a cost of "administrative distancing between central office and school site." Superintendents studied by Bredeson (1995) reported that instructional issues were of the greatest importance, yet most of their time was spent on management. (Also see Glass [1992] and Jackson [1995] on this topic.)

A major problem in school reform emerges. Superintendent socialization and training, their multiple roles and expectations, the uncertainty in determining effectiveness, and the convenience of maintaining status quo norms influence superintendents to be more managers than leaders, less likely to engage in successful change, and more likely to promote only structural-level reform. Yet we need superintendents to leverage district-level support for school improvement. In this chapter, we focus on how a superintendent helped transform a school district into a learning community intent on changing instructional practice in classrooms and improving student outcomes. Our chapter contents are (1) objectives, (2) superintendent as person and professional, (3) district context, (4) case description, and (5) a problem-stimulated task for a work team of prospective superintendents. We constructed the case as a series of dilemmas confronting Jason Kilborne (fictitious name). Kilborne's responses to these dilemmas serve as suggestions for the problem-based learning (PBL) module. After your work team has gathered the required information, you may decide on other feasible alternatives.

Case Objectives Gained through PBL

Aspiring superintendents can:

1. gain a rich context through which problem-solving skills can be applied to superintendents' personal situations;
2. build a knowledge base centered on a major problem defining the superintendency (instructional leadership in the age of accountability); and
3. develop a consistent disposition toward making decisions based on a deeply held set of beliefs about superintendent instructional leadership.

THE SUPERINTENDENT: THE PERSON AND PROFESSIONAL

Jason Kilborne, a forty-seven-year-old white male from the Northeast, resettled in this southeastern state after graduating from a liberal arts college with a degree in German. He taught German and Spanish for three years at a large, metropolitan district before entering administration as an assistant principal (seven years), middle school principal (one year), and high school principal (seven years). In 1987, he became an area superintendent supervising twenty schools and was elevated to acting deputy superintendent (1991–92). Kilborne has a master's and a doctorate in administration; he studied mentors for his dissertation. He is married to an elementary teacher whom he met after college; they have two boys, ages fourteen and seventeen. Kilborne began his superintendency in July 1992.

In early 1992, Kilborne realized that it was time to move on from the huge urban district in which he had spent twenty-five years. The district was too big; no one, according to Kilborne, could make substantial changes in a district with 140 schools. In addition to getting a fresh start, Kilborne had learned in his doctoral program that schools had to change. Having conceptualized the problem of deepseated organization change, Kilborne continued to search for an answer. He read widely (often at 5 A.M.): Schlechty (*Schools for the Twenty-first Century*), Covey (*Seven Habits of Highly Effective People*), Lieberman (*The Work of Restructuring Schools*), and Senge (*The Fifth Discipline*).

He began conceptualizing his ideas in writing: Changing the culture of school and the very nature of schooling requires a monumental shift in thinking, not the mindless application of trivial improvements to the current institution. Public education requires the transformation of our hundred-year-old notions of schooling to build "schools of voice" in which all stakeholders are involved in the democratic process of planning for the continuous improvement of all students. Schools of voice foster a strong sense of community and commonality of purpose within public education. They require stakeholders to model the empowered, entrepreneurial behavior required for student vocational success in the twenty-first century.

His beliefs comprising this framework for change included the following:

- Public education must change.
- People are good and, under the right conditions, can change their practice.
- Practice must be research based.
- Practice must be child focused.
- Personnel unwilling to change their practice should no longer be employed by the district.

How did Kilborne find the right "job fit" between his beliefs and district context?

THE RICHMOND PUBLIC SCHOOLS DISTRICT

Rural Richmond County (with thirty-four thousand people) is located on the coastal plain approximately sixty miles from an interstate highway. The general area had a textile base, now almost nonexistent. Fifty-five percent of the county's sixty-two hundred students (45% minority) are on free/reduced lunch. The area, however, had economic growth potential: large farms, a sizable Coast Guard base, a regional university (enrollment: twenty-three hundred students) and a community college, and plans for a large prison. The county seat (population: fourteen thousand) serves as a regional service center. The annual budget slightly exceeded $30 million in 1992. The district's 350 teachers and 109 classified employees work in one high school, one junior high school, and eight elementary schools. Two assistant superintendents (instruction and administration) and thirteen other administrators comprise the central office. The district recently spent $20 million on capital improvements.

DILEMMA 1: FINDING A DISTRICT WITH THE POTENTIAL FOR DISTRICTWIDE INSTRUCTIONAL IMPROVEMENT

Deciding to leave his district was one thing. Finding a district where Kilborne might implement his game plan was quite another. He set out to find such a district. Not forced to leave his current position, he wanted to find the right match between his instructional vision and district context. In early 1992, five districts made him offers.

During his interview at Richmond County, Kilborne described his game plan. The school board was so impressed with his experience and expertise that Kilborne's biggest problem was convincing the board that he wanted the job. Board members asked, "Why leave a nationally recognized district to come to Richmond?"

After spending two days studying the district, Kilborne realized that this was the district in which he could bring about substantial change, for three reasons. First, Richmond County had a local board committed to school improvement, not to micromanagement. The seven-member school board were mainly professionals (a pediatrician, an engineer, a computer specialist, a community college instructor, an English professor at the local university, a housewife, and a businesswoman) with a shared mission for bringing in a superintendent from the outside with a convincing game plan for improving the district academically. Several board members had grown up in Richmond County and were well connected to the political-economic infrastructure. Kilborne speculated that he could tap their expertise and seek their advice as he contemplated managerial moves and leadership direction. Before accepting the position, Kilborne tested the board's commitment. During his reconnaissance, he had realized that new leadership was needed at one school. He shared confidentially with the board chair, "If I can't move [the principal] out, I'm not coming." Replied the board chair, "Don't worry. We are not into micromanagement. We'll back you."

Second, the Richmond board was under pressure by local business interests to improve the schools. Such an external pressure fit in with Kilborne's orientation as change agent. Changing and improving schools and regional economic competitiveness were interrelated: Status quo administration would not be a districtwide norm at Richmond. It was no accident that Richmond County had limited financial resources but a strong commitment to local funding. As a low-wealth district ranking in the bottom quartile of counties in "Ability to Pay" and the bottom quintile in "Adjusted Property Valuation," it ranked in the top quartile in "Overall Effort." An Outcomes-Based Education grant would provide money for professional development and public relations strategies in focusing the community on the need to establish high academic expectations for its graduates.

Third, his previous central office experience would make this first superintendency equivalent to a lateral entry. He had supervised more schools while area superintendent than there were schools in Richmond County.

Since organization change is an ongoing process, the dilemma of a superintendent impacting instruction would play itself out over his entire career spent at Richmond. However, he had made a good start by using his belief system as a marketing strategy to link up with a district with the potential to make an instructional impact. He firmly believed that there was a good job fit. Now it was up to him to see that instructional change actually happened.

DILEMMA 2: MEETING IMMEDIATE MANAGERIAL CHALLENGES

Kilborne had expected to start immediately on instructional improvement. He soon learned that more pressing fiscal and personnel problems had to be confronted, and confronted very quickly. He spent the first two weeks collecting information and assessing the district's strengths and weaknesses. Board members and most administrators, teachers, parents, community leaders shared their perceptions of district problems.

What he learned was that Richmond County had a $200,000 electrical utilities debt because of a July 1992 58% rate increase. Also in the 1992–93 budget was $500,000 in nonrecurring funds, which the schools would not have next year. Third, Richmond needed another $20 million for building renovation.

In December 1992, Kilborne realized that the schools would have to go to the county commissioners for $800,000 additional money for the 1993–94 budget. (Last year they had received a $75,000 increase.) "If we are not careful, everything we plan to do in school improvement will fall by the wayside if we run out of money." In May 1993, Richmond Schools received a budget increase of $575,000. It also received a commitment of $5 million to convert an elementary school to a middle school.

How did Kilborne and the board pull this off? They used three tactics. The superintendent gathered data to convince commissioners of school needs: "We spent a lot of time with the county commissioners providing them and the general public with the information so no one would rattle their sabers and claim that they did not know about our fiscal needs." Second, Kilborne made sure that the various publics perceived the schools as a major gameplayer within the Richmond County government infrastructure. "No county agency [e.g., firefighters, police] gave more to the United Way than schools."

Third, Kilborne made presentations about the value of the schools at meetings frequented by the local politicians. "I'm aware of the reciprocity—I've got to be interested in what they're doing, if they are going to support me." These meetings included the chamber of commerce, the Lions Club, the Rotary Club, and school functions, such as science fairs and PTA meetings. He was quick to see opportunities for collaboration with community organizations. To his staff he queried, "Can we plug in our outcomes-based education plans for students in community service and somehow meet some needs of chamber of commerce?"

As another managerial problem, termites were discovered in the bus garage. Through cooperation of county commissioners, Richmond County put a successful bid on a building formerly owned by a bankrupt construction company for busses. The crisis was averted.

During this managerial phase, Kilborne set some personnel expectations in successfully pressuring two teachers, two teacher assistants, and two classified employees to resign. One first-year teacher and a second-year teacher (new to the district) both had had poor performance evaluations. There had been questions of moral turpitude about the teaching assistants, although not in scandalous proportions. As the board had promised, the principal in the troubled school alluded to above before Kilborne's arrival had resigned. Kilborne also created a second assistant superintendency (that of instruction) and hired him from outside the district. (Again, no problems from the board.) This administrator became a solid supporter and colleague in Kilborne's organization change efforts.

Despite his mission of making an instructional impact upon a district, Kilborne first had to get his house in order. Because of his administrative experience, Kilborne had the flexibility to put instructional improvement on the back burner for the first six months of his tenure. Kilborne reflected on the crises of his first year: "We're all working together well. I also think that if something happened [an obvious case of neglect or incompetence], district personnel know I'd nail their butts. I clearly communicated that expectation." Given his personnel moves, such an expectation among Richmond School personnel is plausible.

DILEMMA 3: HOW CAN KILBORNE GET THE MESSAGE ACROSS TO PRINCIPALS AND TEACHERS THAT SCHOOLS HAD TO CHANGE?

Managerial moves, even the tough ones in budget and personnel, were not new to Kilborne, who had faced similar problems in the high-stakes metropolitan environment as an area and deputy superintendent. The long-range problem, however, was changing how personnel at Richmond County did business. A major strategy was to get a strong, consistent message for the need to change out there to principals and teachers.

At the opening convocation in his first year, Kilborne made his convictions clear. If public schools were going to provide leadership in the face of impending social chaos, public schools were going to have to change:

> The roles and relationships among district members must change dramatically. Changes in the culture operating in public education will result in learning outcomes in students that make them independent thinkers and problem-solvers capable of working productively with others. These learning outcomes are possible only with the institutionalization of a dramatically different vision of public education, education as a "knowledge-work" organization.

A teacher summed up Kilborne's message:

> One of the things we know is that we can't plan for what our kids' future is going to be because we don't know what that is. . . . You have to teach them to be self-directed learners so that no matter what they are up against they will be able to learn it. They are going to have six to ten different career changes. There is no way to keep up with anything, so you have to be able to give them skills to survive in any environment.

The superintendent described the knowledge-work organization in which the district is the "unit of direction," the school is the "unit of change," and the classroom is the "unit of impact." New roles included the superintendent as the "teacher and communicator of the vision," principals as "leaders of leaders," teachers as "leaders of workers," and students as "apprentice workers" in his vision for public education.

Kilborne also valued research as a basis for change, and this research had to be child focused: "We have spent a lot of time focusing on the importance of research and what does research have to say. We don't want to experiment on kids. We don't want to waste time." He taught and communicated this value consistently in a variety of venues throughout the district. In a speech to district employees, Kilborne modeled the use of research both in framing his analysis of shortcomings of current public school culture and in his prescriptions for future district practices. In a letter to elementary teachers four years later, he congratulated them on their progress in the use of research in their practice. Also willing to "take the heat" for his convictions, the superintendent responded to teachers questioning the authority of a consultant advocating the change of teaching practices: "She speaks with the same authority you do or anybody else does. Her authority rests on her ability to back up what she's saying by research. These things she's talking about—she's made them work in other places."

Kilborne also expressed an emerging impatience with district personnel who resisted change. Believing that district leadership had the responsibility to demonstrate effective practice, he expected district practitioners to adopt practices demonstrably effective with all students. If judged to be incapable of "doing the right thing," personnel resisting change should be replaced. At an administrator retreat the assistant superintendent stressed that principals reinforce the message delivered to teachers new to the district in induction activities. They were not free to come into the district and do things that do not work. This standard also was implicit in the District Values Statement: "Accountability measures must include . . . adult performance." The numerous personnel moves made by Kilborne during the first year backed up this value statement with actions.

Kilborne made sure that he delivered a loud and clear message: Teachers had to change their classroom practices to be successful with all learners. This message had an authenticity because it was backed by the five values comprising Kilborne's beliefs framework. He had the board's support because he had campaigned on the basis of his framework. Kilborne, however, faced a much larger dilemma: How can we provide teachers with the skills they need to provide stimulating, enriching instruction to students?

DILEMMA 4: HOW DO WE GET TEACHERS TRAINED IN STUDENT-CENTERED INSTRUCTION?

Kilborne realized that school change was strewn with failed efforts at school change and staff development. Idealistic pledges usually are made yet nothing happens to impact classrooms. Kilborne was intent on not having this occur in Richmond County. He had learned from previous administrative experience that changing the fundamental structures of schooling is tough work. Schools cannot change unilaterally; they needed support for change.

Kilborne operationalized teacher skill development largely as a mega-problem-solving challenge. He used a sports metaphor to explain the connection among learning, confidence, and motivation:

> It is like taking a team that has never won. How do you motivate the players and give them confidence and pride in themselves? It is getting principals or teachers in touch with things that have worked, making them knowledgeable, creating an environment where everybody is learning, where it is OK not to know, and where there is a lot of support and nurture. That gradually builds confidence, and as you get some successes, the pride builds.

He used four strategies in providing skill development for teachers:

- Supporting change longer be employed by the district
- Utilizing data to support change
- Providing adult learning
- Delegating and mentoring

Kilborne first had to be specific about what behaviors comprised student-centered instruction. In his first speech to district employees, he outlined eleven instructional strategies that would enrich student learning activities. He related them to research and provided concrete examples of classroom applications. He even modeled several strategies during his presentation. Teachers willing to engage in innovative practices were rewarded through district foundation grants, and book clubs were started in which administrators, teachers, and community leaders explored innovative instructional techniques and strategies for implementing them. Demonstrating support for risk-taking behaviors, several board members entertained district personnel in unusual and unexpected ways. They dressed in 1960s costumes and lip-synched songs from the 1960s for members of school improvement teams. Board members risked embarrassing themselves in front of district employees to convey the message that risk in attempting to provide real change in the district is worth the possibility of failure.

The ability to assess instructional practice and programs is critical for an organization in the process of change. Kilborne used data to challenge the thinking of teachers, to identify problems and shape solutions, and to assess progress of district programs and professional growth. He provided this rationale in use of data: "We have created situations that require the adults to learn in this district, and we have done that in many ways. We have challenged people's thinking. They've said, 'Well, this is the way we've always done it,' and we've said, 'Well, is it working? Show us.'"

So using teachers as action researchers collecting data on how students learn is a critical skill. In his speech to district employees, Kilborne used data to frame his analysis and support his conclusions about nontraditional classroom practice. He cited statistics to document the looming international economic crisis and consequences for the American standard of living and education practice. By demanding and using data, the superintendent challenged the thinking of teachers.

Teachers, however, had to learn other problem-solving skills. The superintendent linked adult learning, the development of professional confidence, and the creation of intrinsic motivation. "I think motivation is an intrinsic thing; I don't think it is an extrinsic thing. You try to get people confident." He initiated adult learning strategies, partly by leading professional development sessions and book clubs himself. At one elementary school, a consultant spent the day modeling instruction in various classrooms. Teachers from that school as well as teachers from other schools followed the consultant from classroom to classroom, observing as the consultant demonstrated language arts or math instructional strategies. In another school, teachers from other schools observed colleagues demonstrate instructional strategies built on instruction provided previously by the district consultant.

This superintendent helped set the norm of problem-solving skills in the district partly through a balance of delegating, mentoring, and intervention. On delegating, he reflected, "I do not get in people's way. I believe in hiring people—teaching them, telling them what needs to get done, and then getting out of their way but not telling them, not micromanaging what they are doing." Having provided opportunities for principal discussion of policy documents on delegating decision making to teachers at the retreat, he charged them with the responsibility of developing consensus with their faculties. Kilborne dispersed decision-making responsibilities so that power "comes from giving power to other people."

Kilborne mentored followers experiencing problems with practice: "People want to do what is right and want to do a good job, and I think my role is to help lead or guide them to discover the right answers." The principal at one school asked Kilborne to join his council in helping them decide how to disperse their funds. This principal reported that teachers on the council were terrified at making mistakes. Kilborne expressed faith that teachers and principals were capable of solving their own problems. This did not mean that he failed to intervene when asked or when necessary. Intervention came in the form of assistance rather than retribution. At the same time, he was willing to play hard ball, if necessary. One principal complained that principals were giving too much power away to teachers. Kilborne confronted this principal at an administrators' retreat: "In our group discussion, you had the opportunity to state your opinion. You said nothing, so you have to accept the consequences."

In sum, this superintendent was creating a knowledge-work organization capable of providing for the continuous improvement of all students. Traditional school practice (teachers dispensing decontextualized information down to passive students) cannot prepare students as independent thinkers capable of working productively in collaboration with others. District administrators, principals, and teachers should develop the same skills themselves. Student-centered instruction must be learned by teachers through professional development, school empowerment, and classroom experimentation. By supporting these changes, Kilborne reassured district professionals that they would not be punished for failure as they experimented with new teaching strategies. Failure became a source of learning for the innovative practitioner.

Yet problem-solving skills would not develop through central office efforts alone, such as unilaterally providing professional development and decentralizing decision making. The other major piece was changing the traditional, isolated classroom culture with a collaborative one. This change required a perspective that extended the definition of district organization to include the wider community. This challenge leads to the last dilemma confronting Kilborne.

DILEMMA 5: HOW CAN RICHMOND SCHOOLS CREATE A COLLABORATIVE CULTURE?

Principals and teachers cannot change and acquire essential problem-solving skills for student-centered instruction unless roles and relationships change among all members of the school organization. As informed decision making is vested in the school, the school becomes the "unit of change" capable of continuous improvement. Developing an organization perspective through districtwide expectations, systems of accountability, and policy focuses attention of members on the ultimate goal of the district: succeeding with all students.

Interaction with the wider community provides greater knowledge and support for the district. A collaborative culture within the district and between the organization and the wider community becomes essential to continuous change in the organization. He helped set collaborative norms through four strategies: (1) building the learning capacity of schools, (2) developing communication channels, (3) developing the organization perspective of members, and (4) involving the wider community.

In building the learning capacity of the schools Kilborne commented:

> We talk about building the capacity of people, and we have to build the capacity of schools. What kinds of knowledge and expertise have to reside within a school building for it to be a continuously improving organization?
>
> Building school capacity implied use of site-based management through which school personnel work together to establish new organization structures of collegiality. Only by working collaboratively will teachers find the strength to implement significant change not typically available to the individual practitioner isolated in his or her classroom.
>
> Decisions about what and how to teach need to be made by teams of teachers sharing their best thinking and practice. Increasing collegiality and teacher involvement in decision making are essential norms for building and sustaining long-term commitment to innovation and improvement.

The superintendent developed the decision-making capacity of schools by training school staff in collaborative decision making. All schools in the district had a school improvement team involved in decision making. The district played a role in assessing school improvement plans, which, if necessary, were returned to the school for revision.

Principals played a critical role in developing school capacity. At an administrative retreat the superintendent explained his expectations of principals in presenting drafts of district policies to their faculties. Principals should develop consensus about school policy, and that consensus is only possible with a team approach as a learning organization. Kilborne led his central office in decentralizing decision making to schools through use of councils. Textbook selection, professional development, and various grant funds were channeled directly to the schools.

Second, Kilborne connected collaboration to developing communication channels within the district. He centered communication around the idea of "dialogue," which he defined as encouraging interchange in which two parties are full-fledged participants with influence on the nature of the interaction.

Reinforcing the need for continuing dialogue, the superintendent provided a summary of meetings with elementary teachers and district administrators to discuss a draft of the communication skills policy. He set up a communications skills council with teacher representation from every school.

The superintendent also used both informal and formal communication channels. Informally, the superintendent exhibited management by walking-around behaviors, spending a great deal of time visiting schools and classrooms. He visited classrooms, conversed with teachers, and greeted teachers in hallways.

He described himself as someone who was "pretty easy to get next to, to talk to, regardless of who it is. I communicate all the time. I talk to everybody. I acknowledge that they are there, and their work." In returning people's phone calls, he reassured employees that he was willing to deal with their concerns. Asking questions and listening to followers were means of identifying problems.

The superintendent used formal communication channels in meeting regularly with school administrators and instructional specialists. In assessing the value of such meetings he pinpointed a major problem in how schools are organized:

> Schools have never spent lots of time for reflection. . . . We always spend a lot of time talking about stuff, and we kind of do "What do you think?" and we just sort of shoot the bull. I think that's how you learn and how you process. Really, what we're about is almost reintellectualizing how we do our business. You don't do that overnight, and I think that's an ongoing process.

Formal communication with teacher representatives from every school took place at monthly professional advisory council meetings. Teachers presented the concerns of other teachers about districtwide problems, and the superintendent and teacher representatives developed solutions. The superintendent invigorated the local television education channel to communicate with the community. He also communicated with the public through two monthly newsletters, *From a Place Called School* and *Talk of the Town.*

As a third strategy in developing a collaborative culture, Kilborne used a districtwide organization perspective, including

> getting people to think systematically. All too often we solve one problem and create three more. Folks must see how things are all interrelated. Discipline is an example. You can't change the way you discipline students without changing the way students and teachers relate to one another, the way parents and teachers relate to one another, and the way principals and teachers relate to one another. All that has to be consistent. You don't have a very authoritarian relationship between principal and teachers and then expect teachers to engage kids in class meetings and solve their own problems. That's just not going to happen.

He helped develop the organization perspective through systems of accountability and district policies. The central office developed data indicators that reflect the district's new focus on improved student achievement. Forty-two data indicators were grouped into six categories appropriate to Richmond's vision, including expanded student achievement/outcomes and community and parent involvement.

District policy was developed to help stabilize these organization changes with cultural changes. The superintendent explained the role of district policy:

> I want what we are doing it to last. Any time I have ever tried to do any change, I have always tried to institutionalize it. One way to make sure you change the culture is to implement some policies that will last longer than I as an individual will last. That is not to say that that policy might never be changed but that if it is changed, it will require some sort of thoughtful process.

The last strategy was involving the wider community through efforts to forge stronger links between the organization and parents, between the organization and the business community, and between the organization and social service agencies. The superintendent explained his efforts by saying, "This is not my place. I may move on, but I think the district belongs to the community. It belongs to everybody and my role is trying to help them see how and why it needs to change so that the people of the community can help their kids to be successful."

The success of the schools was linked to the success of the community. The district involved the wider community in the process of district change through the use of public forums and efforts to market the schools to the public through the use of educational television. Kilborne, other central office personnel, and business and community leaders used the OBE grant money to identify through focus groups essential skills that Richmond County students needed to survive in an increasingly competitive global market. These broad skills, in turn, were connected both to the quality indicators of student work and to the state accountability system. This interlocking accountability system provided the glue that connected classrooms to the larger community. This system also provided external pressure for principals and teachers to change and improve their practices.

He also forged links with parents. In one publication, he described the promotion/intervention policy and parents' role in supporting the efforts of their children. This same effort to involve parents in the learning of their children was evident in the district homework policy, which explained how parents could provide successful learning opportunities in the home. Parent-teacher meetings were used to explain changes and the important role of parents in the change process.

Kilborne's concern that the district organization involve parents was evident in the development of the student reassignment plan. Some board members were initially unwilling to grant any exceptions to the proposed plan. The superintendent encountered the views that there might be legitimate reasons for granting exceptions and that failing to allow parents an appeal process would violate the district's efforts to be "more customer oriented." At a school board meeting held at a centrally located school rather than the board office to provide more space, parents dissatisfied with the district reassignment plan voiced their concerns. The board decided to delay its decision on school reassignment until the spring to afford more opportunity for community input. A further delay in implementation of the reassignment plan was evidenced by revisions of plans to open the new middle school, scheduled for the next school year. Rather than force through the district's reassignment plan, the new school would merely split the seventh and eighth grade populations between the two middle schools. School redistricting awaits community consensus.

Kilborne also forged stronger links with the business community and community agencies. Business leaders helped produce a video based on interviews with community employers who explained the world of work awaiting high school graduates. This video was played on the education channel. He made presentations to groups like the Lions and Rotary Clubs on defining OBE clearly and garnering support for the project. "I was on our TV channel to talk up our forum and exit outcomes," he remarked. The superintendent also shaped business support by describing ways in which local business could support education by supporting family involvement with the schools. He discussed linkage between the social service agencies and the schools. The district document, "A Community of Achievement," described efforts to involve government agencies, such as the Department of Social Services and the local office of the District Health Department.

In connecting the wider community to the standards of quality through the OBE grant and to collaborative efforts, Kilborne gained political protection. When informed that a neighboring superintendent was fired because she tried to ramrod similar instructional changes in her district, Kilborne responded, "She was setting herself up. One thing you have to do is test community reaction to what you are doing. If they oppose it, wait and try to educate them about why you are proposing change. Otherwise, you will cut your throat."

As informed decision making was vested at the school level, the school became the unit of change capable of continuous improvement. As members of the organization begin to share their experience with successful practice, they become a source of knowledge and support for one another. Developing an organization perspective through districtwide expectations, a system of accountability, and policy focused attention of members on the goal of the organization: succeeding with all students. District interaction with the wider community provided greater support for the district. A collaborative culture within the organization and between the organization and the wider community becomes essential to continuous change in the district.

CONCLUSION AND UNIQUE ASPECTS OF THIS CASE

Kilborne put into practice the balance between district centralization and school autonomy advocated by reformers such as Fullan. This superintendent and central office personnel, supported by the local board, provided rationale for change and supported change efforts through professional development, site-based management, and enabling policies. How many superintendents conduct professional development activities to their own teachers? The community helped set the districtwide exit expectations for high school graduates. Teachers then developed indicators of quality student work. Finally, schools were given the autonomy to make decisions crafted to helping their own students achieve the quality standards. Centralization and decentralization efforts, in sum, were connected through a joint emphasis on improving school learning conditions for principals, teachers, and students. The goal was focused on improving student learning outcomes.

Kilborne was successful because he first developed a well-grounded belief system about how schools could change and improve. He marketed his belief system repackaged as a school improvement game plan to local boards and found the right "job fit." He then articulated his beliefs to various constituencies throughout the district. Last, he connected his belief system to actions.

Regarding this connection, a teacher described the importance of the instructional specialist to the development of the learning capacity of the school, the thinking behind it, and Kilborne's role in the creation of this position:

> The most important thing is to cut the classroom size and have as few students as possible. . . . So it was a biggie for the county to say, "We're not going to give you any more people, but we are going to take one of your lead teachers, someone that is strong in curriculum and people skills, and we're going to designate that person the instructional specialist." They didn't pull these people in from elsewhere; they took our own teachers and made them instructional specialists. Dr. Kilborne was in charge of that. This specialist is always available when I need help with reading or writing or communication skills. So the door is wide open.

The reader might notice that Kilborne seemed completely fearless in meetings with teacher groups, media, community groups, and so forth. He even led book clubs on changing the expectations and policies of U.S. schooling. Perhaps he was fearless because his actions were so closely tied to his belief system. He developed a consistency between actions and words.

What evidence is there that Kilborne was successful in increasing student outcomes during his four-year tenure? Student outcomes improved from 1993 to 1998. Grades 3–8 reading and mathematics, for instance, improved by six and nine scaled points, respectively (scale: 1–100). Kilborne was named the Superintendent of the Year in 1996 by the state school boards association. Also in 1996 Kilborne received the Governor's Entrepreneurial School System Award.

YOUR PROBLEM-STIMULATED TASK

Kilborne developed his belief system through his reading and writings, including an article in *Phi Delta Kappan*. Other outstanding school leaders have read and written to develop personal game plans for action. (See, e.g., Keedy & Finch [1992] about a principal who helped implement shared decision making with teachers in a rural high school.)

Your problem-stimulated learning challenge is to construct a professional beliefs package connected to an action plan that is to be tested out before a local board searching for a superintendent such as Jason Kilborne. Kilborne might appear to be a "model" for prospective superintendents to consider when constructing a game plan for instructional improvement.

LEARNING ACTIVITIES

Here are suggested steps and group roles useful in accomplishing your task:

1. All group members read appropriate sections of Bridges and Hallinger's (1992) *Problem-Based Learning for Administrators* related to problem-stimulated learning (particularly pp. 1–12 and 134–143).
2. Your first subtask is to construct a meaningful context within which a reasonably authentic board interview might occur. Consult Louis and Miles (1992)] for the urban context, Keedy and Allen (1998) for the rural context, and Chapman (1997) for both contexts.
3. A team member then observes several meetings of a local board to collect information for board member profiles (see Bridges & Hallinger [1992], pp. 139–140). Consult Keedy and Allen (1998) for a discussion of a superintendent and central office that obstructed the instructional improvement efforts of an elementary school.
4. Another team member interviews the board chair with anonymity assured to find out the collective orientation of this board toward expectations for

the new superintendent. Consult Keedy and Freeman (1997) for a board chair perspective toward school restructuring.

5. The entire group then constructs both the board profiles and the administrative context within which the new superintendent would work. Kilborne's case merely exemplifies a context. Your own context is based on the information collected by your team members in steps 2–5.

6. A group member calls the state board association and obtains several board evaluations for superintendent interviews. The group chooses the one most appropriate to the context established earlier.

7. Using the Kilborne case and your own case context, identify a series of administrative dilemmas confronting the new superintendent. These dilemmas must be consistent with the context. Your district, for instance, may be urban and large or small and suburban. The board members, their profiles, and the board chair's expectations also must be factored into the composition of these dilemmas. Kilborne's dilemmas "fit" his context. Your dilemmas may be entirely different, given your context.

8. Your next subtask is to construct a simulated first-year superintendent. First, write a beliefs package from the literature on the superintendency and school change and improvement. (For sample sources, see References section.) Again, the beliefs of Kilborne should be merely a guide, not a template, for this subtask. One team member should coordinate the development of an outline and gradual integration of additional readings into a cohesive, persuasive beliefs package. Finally, write a résumé consistent with this beliefs package.

9. The entire team identifies a nearby superintendent reputed for his or her instructional leadership. Query this superintendent about these belief statements. Adjust them, when necessary, so that they are consistent with this superintendent.

10. A team member then interviews this superintendent as to what actions he or she might take in addressing these administrative dilemmas.

11. Now for the third subtask: the board interview. One member plays the role of a prospective, first-year superintendent who will present his candidacy based on the professional beliefs package and action plan prepared by the group.

12. Another member sets the scene within the entire classroom. This person cajoles and, if necessary, "volunteers" other class members to play the roles of board members and to act consistently with the assigned board profile. The board also is given copies of the prospective candidate's beliefs statements, a résumé, and the administrative dilemmas, but not the actions taken projected by the interviewed superintendent.

13. The ensuing simulated interview between the superintendent and board is videotaped to provide information useful to the entire class in critiquing interviewing skills.

14. Students not playing the parts of the board or team should use the evaluation sheets in assessing whether (a) the board should make an offer to the candidate and reasons for this decision and (b) the candidate should accept the offer, if made. Given the observed interactions of the board meeting, is there perceived a reasonable "job fit"?

PRODUCTS

There are five products to this problem-simulated task:

- The videotaped interview
- A beliefs package of an ideal instructional leader tempered by the interviewed superintendent
- Responses to the administrative dilemmas by a seasoned superintendent savvy in instructional leadership skills
- A résumé of this prospective superintendent
- Feedback from the class jurors in assessing the interview process

REFERENCES

Bredeson, P. V. (1995, April). *Superintendents' Roles in Curriculum Development and Instructional Leadership: Instructional Visionaries, Collaborators, Supporters, and Delegators.* Paper presented at the annual meeting of the American Educational Research Association, San Francisco.

Bridges, E. M., and Hallinger, P. (1992). *Problem-Based Learning for Administrators.* Eugene, OR: ERIC Clearinghouse on Educational Management, University of Oregon.

Carroll, J. M. (1990). "The Copernican Plan: Restructuring the American High School." *Phi Delta Kappan* 71: 358–365.

Chapman, C. H. (Ed.). (1997). *Beginning Superintendents and the Challenges of Leadership.* New York: Prentice Hall.

Crowson, R. L., and Morris, V. C. (1990). *The Superintendency and School Leadership.* Champaign-Urbana, IL: National Center for School Leadership.

Cuban, L. (1984). "Transforming the Frog into a Prince: Effective Schools Research, Policy, and Practice at the District Level." *Harvard Educational Review* 54: 129–151.

———. (1989). "The District Superintendent and the Restructuring of Schools: A Realistic Appraisal." In T. J. Sergiovanni and J. H. Moore (Eds.), *Schooling for Tomorrow: Directing Reforms to Issues That Count* (pp. 251–271). Boston: Allyn and Bacon.

Fullan, M. G., and Stiegelbauer, S. (1991). *The New Meaning of Educational Change.* New York: Teachers College Press.

Glass, T. E. (1992). *The Study of the American School Superintendency '92: America's Education Leaders in a Time of Reform.* Arlington, VA: American Association of School Administrators.

Glickman, C. D. (1990a). "Open Accountability for the '90s: Between the Pillars." *Educational Leadership* 47(7): 38–42.

————. (1990b). "Pushing School Reform to a New Edge: The Seven Ironies of School Empowerment." *Phi Delta Kappan* 72: 68–75.

Jackson, B. L. (1995). *Balancing Act: The Political Role of the Urban School Superintendent.* Washington, D.C.: Joint Center for Political and Economic Studies.

Johnson, S. M. (1996). *Leading to Change: The Challenge of the New Superintendency.* San Francisco: Jossey-Bass.

Keedy, J. L. (1997). "Don: Breaking the Mold by Reading at Dawn." In C. H. Chapman (Ed.), *Becoming a Superintendent: Challenges of School District Leadership* (pp. 147–160). Upper Saddle River, NJ: Prentice Hall.

Keedy, J. L., and Allen, J. (1998). "Examining District Norms from a Rural School's Site-Based Improvement Perspective: Complementary or Obstructive?" *Journal of School Leadership* 8: 187–210.

Keedy, J. L., and Finch, A. M. (1994). "Examining Teacher-Principal Empowerment: An Analysis of Power." *Journal of Research and Development in Education* 27: 154–166.

Keedy, J. L., and Freeman, E. (1997, March). *School Board Chair Understandings about School Restructuring: Implications for School District Policy.* Paper presented at the annual meeting of the American Educational Research Association, Chicago.

Keedy, J. L., Seeley, D. S., and Bitting, P. (1995). "Leadership Candidate Construction of Normative Frameworks for Principal Preparation Programs: Implications for Fundamental Reform." *Educational Considerations* 23: 6–10.

Louis, K. S., and Miles, M. B. (1990). *Improving the Urban High School.* New York: Teachers College Press.

Mefford, E., and Adkison, J. (1995, April). *Transformational Leadership and the Superintendency: A Case Study.* Paper presented at the annual meeting of the American Educational Research Association, San Francisco.

Schlechty, P. C. (1990). *Schools for the Twenty-first Century.* San Francisco: Jossey-Bass.

11

How Does Merit Pay Create Tension between the Superintendent and the School Board?

Flora Ida Ortiz and Mary G. Mend

BACKGROUND INFORMATION

Conflict between the superintendent and school board is a common theme addressed by researchers and faced by practitioners (Alvey & Underwood, 1985; Arnez, 1981; Blumberg, 1985; Bryant & Grady, 1990; Cuban, 1985; Goldman, 1990; Grady & Bryant, 1991; Hayden, 1987; Lutz & Iannaccone, 1978; Meyer, 1983; Natale, 1990; Sizemore, 1981; Tallerico, 1991). Conflict arises for many reasons, but one of them is that the superintendent is accountable to more than one boss or supervisor. The superintendent is likely to have from five to seven board members who hold him or her accountable. Any one of the members or a number of members can unite to challenge the superintendent on any issue or action.

In the literature, this issue has been most cogently captured through Callahan's (1962) use of the concept of vulnerability. Parker (1996, p. 64) states:

> A condition termed vulnerability occurs, according to Callahan, when a superintendent operates as a scholar pressing for educational excellence. A widely accepted school of thought holds that as a result of this vulnerability, superintendents must also be prepared to be mobile; superintendent vulnerability and mobility are inextricably linked.

Callahan first presented this thesis in *Education and the Cult of Efficiency* where in the preface he wrote, "What was unexpected was the extent, not only of the power of the business-industrial groups, but of the business ideology in the American culture on the one hand and the extreme weakness and vulnerability of schoolmen, [superintendents], on the other" (pp. vii–viii). The combination of these two aspects of the vulnerability of the superintendent reveals the potential for tension between the desire for educational excellence and the current emphasis on efficiency. School board members may differ on their emphasis on either educational excellence or efficiency.

This case reveals a situation in which the superintendent and some board members are pressing for educational excellence, while other board members are calling especially for efficiency. Efficiency in this case is sought from the nonteaching support staff. Some board members want to institute a merit pay plan for the staff to reward employee performance.

In determining how to respond in this case, the superintendent needs to determine how merit pay plans may affect the delivery of educational excellence. How can this issue be addressed to avoid conflict and what are some alternatives to preserve a balance between the provision of educational excellence and efficient and effective employee performance?

KEY AREAS FOR REFLECTION

1. The relationships between school boards and superintendents
2. The relationships between school board members
3. The ethical, legal, social, political, and professional dimensions of board membership
4. Conflict avoidance strategies
5. Scope of the superintendent's responsibilities and authority
6. Knowledge and skills in interpersonal relationships, employee-employer relationships, merit pay plans, and other reward and incentive systems

THE CASE

The School District and the School Board

Mariposa Unified School District (MUSD) is a medium-sized urban school district drawing from the capital city's professional, political, and foreign service and market trading groups. A secondary school and three elementary schools have a total of fifteen thousand students. The area is a cosmopolitan, financial, and political center which experiences growth and turnover simultaneously. The students are from the area, as well as from other countries. Parents are merchants, professionals, or governmental appointees and employees.

The school board consists of seven members who are elected to represent certain geographic areas and groups. When the superintendent was hired, the board consisted primarily of professionals. During her tenure of three years, the composition of the board has changed, so that currently, three out of the seven board members are business executives. It is anticipated that the membership of the board will continue to change and most likely, the proportion of members drawn from the business world will increase. In general, this board is an enlightened one, with commitment to providing excellent education to the youth, and the superintendent enjoys a professional relationship with each member.

The board is divided on the subject of merit pay. They are divided according to their experience with the practice. The businessmen have used merit pay and have been themselves paid accordingly. The female board members have worked in service jobs and have not experienced these systems in the workplace or have had negative experiences. The businessmen are convinced that merit pay will improve performance among support staff. Their experience is the basis for this conviction. For example, the current president of the school board is director of an international educational institute. The former president retired from his business when he became board president, and the third is president of a major manufacturing firm. All of these individuals obtained graduate business degrees from outstanding universities. All of them have school-age children. With the exception of the president of the manufacturing firm, the two male board members manage small groups of employees and their relationship to their employees is that of manager versus worker. The fourth male board member is a business consultant who travels extensively and was just made partner of an international company. His education includes an MBA from a prestigious business school, and even though he works independently, his business orientation is strongly influenced by his training and his work.

From this brief description of the board members' training and experience, we can see how the conviction to impose merit pay for school staff originates. For example, one board member relating his personal experience claimed that after some adjustment, he now "loves merit pay." Another board member explained, "Many a mediocre employee turned around and became much more productive." Still, another board member derisively laughed as he said, "Around here, you have to wait to get your reward in heaven."

The female board members differ in that they have not obtained degrees in business. One of the members has been a teacher, owned a kindergarten, but is presently retired and involved in philanthropic activities. Another of the female members has degrees in architectural studies and philosophy. Her work experience includes managing a merit pay system for nurses at a general hospital for two years. Finally, the third female member is self-employed in a medical clinic with her doctor husband. These females do not believe in the merit pay system, as do the males. For example, they referred to the time it took to supervise and the kind of atmosphere merit pay created. One of them said, "Teachers would never accept the idea because it is so foreign to the culture of educators." In general, they express the view that a service organization is not a place for merit pay systems where every act or service is linked to money. Employees who do not receive the merit pay award feel justified in pointing to the ones who do when some special or disagreeable task is before them. The practical issue is that sometimes there is no money for all who perform well and when there is, the amount is not high enough to be much of an incentive. Others do not want to look like they care or that they might need the extra money while others resent being overlooked when they believe their work is not appreciated.

The Superintendent

The superintendent's education, in contrast, includes an undergraduate degree in English/speech from a prestigious state university and a doctorate in education from an equally high-status private university. With the exception of working as a secretary during her college years, the superintendent has been in education all of her life working as an urban high school teacher, principal, central office official, and superintendent.

Dr. Victoria March is completing the third year of a four-year contract at MUSD. Her previous job was as superintendent of a large urban school district. She was successful in transforming the district from one in bankruptcy, constant administrator turnover, and deteriorating student performance records to a stable district where student performance rose and is now viewed as a desirable district in which to work. Her success with that district led to her employment with MUSD, where she is highly regarded. Only twice has this district had a woman as acting head for a one-year period each.

The Problem

March leads a district where student performance is high, parents and school personnel are supportive, and the school board has respected professional autonomy amongst the faculty. The election two years ago of new members tipped the make-up of the school board of education to a majority from business. At the same time, a businessman was elected president and another elected treasurer. They have increasingly called for business practices and procedures in the management of the school district. For example, they have examined business office procedures, work flow, equipment and records. Personnel records and employee performance have become topics of inquiry and discussion. These actions were undertaken by a subcommittee headed by the board treasurer and strongly supported by the board president.

The committee's inspection resulted in some board members' dissatisfaction with the support staff. The general view is that the school should never pay more than the average salary for the same job in the community. Several board members believe the salaries of the school's support staff are high and their performance is low.

The superintendent and board members responded to this report by hiring a consultant to compare school district salaries with salaries for comparable jobs in the community. Salary comparisons were made to businesses having similar budgets and number of employees. The volume of sales in some businesses was equated with the school district's annual budget for use in the study. The job categories studied included maintenance and skilled trades, bus drivers, gardeners, secretaries, clerks, data processors, and accountants—a total of approximately four hundred employees. The consultant reported that school district salaries were low, very low, or on the low side of average. Twenty persons appeared to be overpaid in their job categories compared with the market study.

The board members who favor merit pay then asked the superintendent to contrast the length of the school day and school year with "business" hours and "business" vacations to determine the accuracy of the comparisons. This analysis showed
that half of the school jobs under review were eight-hour assignments. Based on a
proportion of the day and year worked by the other half, it was determined that in
comparison to full-time community job holders, school district employees worked
77% of the time. The subcommittee recommended and the board agreed that school
salaries would be paid at 100% of the average paid for the same eight-hour job in
the community. Five-, six-, or seven-hour jobs would be compensated proportion-
ately. The subcommittee also recommended that all office personnel be assigned to
work eight hours per day exclusive of lunch. The compensation review of support
staff positions during this period yielded substantial corrections, standardization, and
increased support for the new personnel director. Job titles, qualifications, hours,
and work year were made uniform. The number of job groups was reduced and
supervisors were clearly designated. Job descriptions were updated. Differences in
pay were justified or eliminated.

In spite of the changes made, after six months of meeting every two or three weeks,
some board members remained concerned about the nonexistent relationship between pay and performance. These members claimed that there was no incentive to
do excellent work. "Some employees," they remarked, "must be carrying a heavier
load than others. It happens everywhere."

The superintendent was caught in the middle of a split board. She felt that although personally opposed to merit pay in school districts, she had the obligation
to implement a merit pay system for employees if the board so directed. The many
meetings throughout the school year brought many procedural improvements, but
the topic of merit pay was dividing the staff and creating a poor work environment.
The superintendent held to the idea that a few board members could not direct her.
She continued to insist that the whole board discuss the issue of merit pay for support staff and arrive at an agreement as a whole board. She also wanted the board
to approve a salary increase to the support staff before the school year was over.
Budget time approached, and it was time to consider raises for all school district
employees for the following school year.

Salary increases for the following year were granted to the support staff and faculty. Several conditions were attached: (1) teachers would receive their increase in
September, and the support staff would receive theirs in February; (2) raises might
be different amounts for different groups of employees; and (3) salaries for the same
job would not be higher than in the community. With the support and concilia-
tory approach of the board members to consolidate agreement and identify issues
for future board discussion and decision, the superintendent prepared a summary
of the year's accomplishments and recommendations.

For the supporters of merit pay, the task still remains to discuss, understand, vote
for merit pay, and implement it for support staff. For the superintendent, the goal
is to discuss and defeat merit pay, keep the board together, and keep her job. Meet-

ings have started again and the focus is evaluation of employee performance. The superintendent's responsibility is to explain the evaluation process. In reviewing the current practice of evaluation, it was noted that while pay was temporarily withheld for persons on probation, there was no provision to augment pay for employees who worked beyond standard. For board members supporting merit pay, merit pay is seen as the answer. This would provide extra money for all, including teachers. In time, this system is expected to include all supervisors, directors, and principals, resulting in dramatically improved productivity.

The superintendent, after months of discussions and wrestling with merit pay, has come to realize the board and she will never be able to convince each other. She explains:

> Our views and solid positions are based in our various successful careers and personal/ professional value systems. There was their management view that merit pay could not succeed if they could not persuade me that merit pay was the way to go with the gardeners, maintenance men, skilled tradesmen, and secretaries. There was also much anger because I did not do what I was being told they wanted. They were always polite though insistent.

This particular district has no workers' union. Sometimes workers are mobilized for a time, but the historical pattern has been that the leaders are bought off easily and the workers are exploited. The board members who make up the board are familiar with these types of relationships. The culture of business is patriarchic and workers do not have a voice in running the company.

March conceives of schools as service organizations staffed by professionals who relate to each other as colleagues or equals. Her working class background and her experience as a school management negotiator opposite school employee unions had a powerful influence on her interest in and position with respect to the issue of merit pay in schools. She explains:

> Consciously or unconsciously at different times, I very much felt kinship with the workers in school. These workers are sometimes referred to as "*gente obediente,*" people who obey. I felt personal opposition as a minority person with white management, with management men as a woman. Working for five years as a secretary while in college, I remember one of the men saying, "We don't need someone who is too comfortable in the culture; we need someone who can come in, take charge and get the efficiencies we want."
>
> He might have been referring to me, but I didn't hear it that way at the time. Finally, I would add that because of my experience as a school district labor negotiator on the management side opposite teachers as well as support personnel, I know worker concerns. When union negotiators come to the table opposite management negotiators, they come as equals not beggars. School unions have bargained and won rights to a voice in policy making, working conditions, benefits, as well as salary. I am not accustomed to the unilateral management decisions which are so common and so detrimental to the workers here.

The superintendent based many of her arguments against merit pay on two books, *Punished by Rewards: The Trouble with Gold Stars, Incentive Plans, $'s, A's, Praises, and Other Bribes,* by Alfie Kohn, (1993) and *The Will to Lead,* by Marvin Bower (1997). As a management consultant for sixty years and founder of the McKensie Company, Bower centers his discussion on the value of teams, his belief that monetary incentives obstruct creativity and productivity, and conviction that people should be paid according to their performance. His work has been useful to March's defense against a merit pay system in MUSD. Unfortunately, Bower's emphasis is on the educated professionals in business and not the bottom-level workers in nonprofit organizations such as are presented in this case.

THE CHALLENGE

The issue of merit pay could never be discussed by the board and superintendent as a matter of research either in management or in education but as a matter of control. The board members kept referring to the need to "keep staff people at the top of their form, on edge, or competitive with one another spurred on by rewards for employees and supervisors up the line to include management." Analyze the superintendent's and school board members' actions and beliefs. How would you go about avoiding conflict over the issue of merit pay for support staff? What is your advice to the superintendent?

KEY ISSUES AND QUESTIONS

1. What actions are necessary before merit pay is implemented in MUSD?
2. In this case, what are the advantages and disadvantages of having a split board regarding merit pay?
3. What are the characteristics of merit pay that makes it undesirable or inappropriate for school districts?
4. What are the characteristics of merit pay that makes it desirable or appropriate for school districts?

REFERENCES

Alvey, D., and Underwood, K. (1985). "When Boards and Superintendents Clash, It Is over the Balance of Power." *American School Board Journal* 172 (10): 21–25.

Arnez, N. L. (1981). *The Besieged School Superintendent: A Case Study of School Superintendents-School Board Relations in Washington, DC, 1973–1975.* Washington, D.C.: University of America Press.

Blumberg, A., with Blumberg, P. (1985). *The School Superintendent: Living with Conflict.* New York: Teachers College, Columbia University.

Bower M. (1997). *The Will to Lead.* Cambridge, MA: Harvard Business School Press.

Bryant, M., and Grady, M. (1990). "Where Boards Cross the Line." *American School Board Journal* 177 (10): 20–21.

Callahan, R. E. (1962). *Education and the Cult of Efficiency: A Study of the Social Forces That Have Shaped the Administration of the Public Schools.* Chicago: University of Chicago Press.

Cuban, L. (1985). "Conflict and Leadership in the Superintendency." *Phi Delta Kappan* 67(1): 28–30.

Goldman, J. (1990). "Who's Calling the Plays?" *School Administrator* 47 (11): 8–16.

Grady, M., and Bryant, M. (1991) "School Board Presidents Describe Critical Incidents with Superintendents" *Journal of Research in Rural Education* 7 (3): 51–58.

Hayden, J. (1987). "Superintendent-Board Conflict: Working It Out." *Education Digest* 52(8): 11–13.

Kohn, A. (1993). *Punished by Rewards: The Trouble with Gold Stars, Incentive Plans, $'s, A's, Praise, and Other Bribes.* New York: Houghton Mifflin.

Lutz, F. W., and Iannaccone, L. (1978). *Public Participation in Local School Districts.* Lexington, MA: Lexington Books.

Meyer, R. (1983). "How to Handle a Board Member Who Wants to Play His Own Game." *American School Board Journal* 170(11): 27–29.

Natale, J. (1990). "School Board Ethics: On Thin Ice?" *American School Board Journal* 177(10): 16–19.

Parker, R. (1996). "Superintendent Vulnerability and Mobility." *Peabody Journal of Education* 7 (2): 64–77.

Sizemore, B. A. (1981). *The Ruptured Diamond: The Politics of the Decentralization of the District of Columbia Public Schools.* Washington, D.C.: University Press of America.

Tallerico, M. (1991). "School Board Member Development: Implications for Policy and Practice." *Planning and Changing* 22(2): 94–107.

Appendix

ARTIFACT 1. PINEVILLE SCHOOLS CENTRAL OFFICE STAFF

Superintendent of Schools
Finance Officer
Assistant Superintendent for Education Services
Assistant Superintendent for Administrative Services
Assistant Superintendent for Operations
Director of Elementary Instruction
Director of Secondary Instruction
Coordinator of Exceptional Children Services
Coordinator of Testing
Coordinator of Technology

ARTIFACT 2. *TIMES OUTLOOK:* "HOW PINEVILLE STACKS UP"

The state released the latest SEP results Wednesday. Students in grades three through eight took reading and math tests; grades four and seven also took writing tests. In the lists below, the second column shows the overall percentage of students performing at or above grade level on all tests administered at that school.

Exemplary Schools: Strong Academic Improvement

These schools sharply exceeded the state's expectations on test score improvement.

Bear County

Bethel Elementary	74.7
East Middle	66.4
Ellenville Elementary	80.1

Sugar Peach Elementary	86.3
West Elementary	73.9

Caldwell County

Balls Creek Elementary	70.7
Blackburn Elementary	77.8
Caldwell Middle	73.1
Jacobs Ford Elementary	81.5
Oak Hill Elementary	78.8
Viewmont Elementary	77.5

Leighton County

Belmont Elementary	82.6
Belmont Middle	76.5
Erwin Middle	76.7
Costner Elementary	67.5
Henderson Elementary	64.6
North Elementary	63.1
Oakboro Elementary	83.2
Page Elementary	71.3
Shiloh Elementary	90.5
Weddington Elementary	91.9
Woodleaf Elementary	73.7

Pineville City

Clover River Elementary	76.0
Rocky Creek Elementary	85.3
Riverview Middle	71.4

Schools That Met Expectations

These schools reached their goals for improving scores.

Bear County

Burns Middle	68.8
Central Elementary	54.2
Mountain View Elementary	52.8
Sweetwater Elementary	60.8

Caldwell County

Grove Elementary	68.8
Falls Elementary	70.4
Reid Middle	69.9

Leighton County

Briar Creek Elementary	53.8
Ironton Elementary	71.0
Rock Springs Elementary	75.6
Coolwood Middle	70.5

Pineville City
Hickory Hill Elementary   60.4

Schools That Didn't Meet Expectations

These schools did not reach their goals for improving scores but had at least half of their students performing proficiently on tests.

Caldwell County
Liberty Middle   67.9

Leighton County
Jefferson Elementary   60.0
Parkwood Middle   70.5

Pineville City
Central Middle   51.0
Waterford Elementary   52.0

Low-Performing Schools

These schools did not reach their goals for improving scores and had significantly less than 50 percent of students scoring proficiently on tests.

Pineville City
GreenValley Elementary   48.1
Washington Elementary   47.7

ARTIFACT 3. LOW-PERFORMING SCHOOLS DATA

Green Valley Elementary

Category	Student Performance Achievement Level Percentages			
	Level I	Level II	Level III	Level IV
Composite of Reading, Mathematics, Writing	14.50	36.80	36.70	12.00
American Indian Females	0	100	0	0
American Indian Males	0	33.30	66.70	0
Asian Females	10.00	40.00	30.00	20.00
Asian Males	13.60	27.30	40.90	18.20
Black Females	18.70	42.90	32.90	5.50
Black Males	24.90	45.30	26.30	3.60
Hispanic Females	11.10	66.70	22.20	0
Hispanic Males	28.60	57.10	14.30	0
White Females	6.40	28.10	44.50	21.10
White Males	7.50	28.50	45.00	19.00
Multi-Racial Females	0	50.00	50.00	0

Washington Elementary

	Student Performance Achievement Level Percentages			
Category	Level I	Level II	Level III	Level IV
Composite of Reading, Mathematics, Writing	15.00	36.40	33.30	15.30
American Indian Males	50.00	0	16.70	33.30
Asian Females	0	0	69.20	30.80
Asian Males	0	13.30	46.70	40.00
Black Females	14.40	43.80	34.20	7.60
Black Males	28.20	43.90	24.50	3.30
Hispanic Females	12.50	87.50	0	0
Hispanic Males	38.90	38.90	22.20	0
Multi-Racial Females	0	16.70	66.70	16.70
Multi-Racial Males	28.60	14.30	42.90	14.30
White Females	4.40	28.10	38.20	29.40
White Males	7.80	25.00	36.60	30.60
Other Females	33.30	0	66.70	0
Other Males	0	50.00	50.00	0

ARTIFACT 4. LOW-PERFORMING SCHOOLS DATA: STUDENT ACHIEVEMENT, ONE YEAR'S GROWTH

Green Valley Elementary

Subject	Grade	Growth Expected	Actual % Growth	Students At or Above Grade Level
Reading	3	3.8	2.8	44.8
	4	2.8	3.1	52.8
	5	3.0	2.5	55.5
Math	3	5.3	3.9	41.6
	4	6.9	7.4	51.3
	5	5.6	3.8	49.5
Writing	4			32.9

Washington Elementary

Subject	Grade	Growth Expected	Actual % Growth	Students At or Above Grade Level
Reading	3	3.5	2.6	48.6
	4	3.2	2.7	51.5
	5	3.2	2.5	55.7

(*continued*)

Subject	Grade	Growth Expected	Actual % Growth	Students At or Above Grade Level
Math	3	5.3	4.9	45.2
	4	6.5	4.4	46.9
	5	5.1	5.0	51.1
Writing	4			36.2

ARTIFACT 5. GREEN VALLEY AND WASHINGTON SCHOOLS: OTHER DEMOGRAPHIC DATA

Green Valley Elementary School

African-American Students	56.0%
Asian	2.1%
Hispanic	1.8%
White	40.2%
Special Education Students	22.0%
Academically Gifted Students	11.7%

Washington Elementary School

African-American Students	50.8%
Asian	2.3%
Hispanic	0.7%
White	46.2%
Special Education Students	15.0%
Academically Gifted Students	6.1%

ARTIFACT 6. FINANCIAL DATA FOR AREA SCHOOL DISTRICTS

School System Local Revenues	Wealth Per Student Per Student	Spending
Bear County	$1,773	$874
Caldwell County	$1,898	$920
Leighton County	$3,467	$1,464
Pineville City	$4,471	$2,131
State Average	$2,748	$1,424

In addition to spending from local tax sources, the state board of education distributes money to local schools based primarily on student enrollment, but also on other factors such as size and economic need. For example:

- Systems are allocated a certain number of positions to hire teachers, guidance counselors, assistant principals and instructional support, based on student enrollment. Every school gets a principal's position.

- Every system gets a base amount for staff development. Additional money is allocated based on head count.
- Regardless of size, every system is allocated money for a minimum of six central office positions, such as superintendent and transportation director. Money for additional administrators is based on student enrollment.
- Systems receive money for children with special needs based on head count.
- Money for transportation is based on factors such as how far buses must travel.
- Money for at-risk children and alternative schools is based on a system's number of poor children, plus its overall enrollment.
- Money is set aside for poor or small county school systems. City systems are not eligible for that money.

On the average, about 70 percent of the funding comes from the state, 23 percent from local government, and 7 percent from the federal government. Federal money pays for such things as meals for poor children, programs for disadvantaged children and children with special needs, and vocational education. State money pays for most of a school system's staff, plus supplies, equipment, textbooks, staff development, and transportation. Local money pays for school construction, maintenance, new initiatives and programs, and additional educators.

ARTIFACT 7. STATE ASSISTANCE TEAM INFORMATION: AGREEMENT PLAN

As a teacher:

I will accept the responsibility, ownership, and control of the teaching and learning process.
I will be prepared daily.
I will seek knowledge and resources needed for student achievement.
I will constantly assess my students and base instruction on students' needs.
I will collaborate with grade level colleagues and other coworkers to align the curriculum.

As an assistance team member:

I will provide staff development aligned with the school improvement plan.
I will monitor, evaluate, and provide feedback in the school improvement process.
I will encourage empowerment of staff through utilization of school-based management practices and philosophies.
I will work collaboratively with staff, students, parents, and community to increase achievement and performance.
I will assist in identifying, locating, and gathering resources that support a strong instructional program, and that address the needs of a diverse school population.

ARTIFACT 8. ASSISTANCE TEAM ACTIVITIES

Here are some of the things we will be doing at this school as a state assistance team.

Observe the school environment to identify strengths and areas in need of improvement (climate, scheduling, physical features of the building, community involvement strategies).

Confer with school personnel to identify strengths and areas in need of improvement.

Assist in determining and delivering appropriate staff development (in-service to support instruction).

Analyze test data (data collection and analysis).

Provide demonstration lessons and assist staff members in applying effective instructional practices—feedback, monitoring, locating resources, new instructional strategies.

Evaluate, at least semiannually, school personnel and make recommendations concerning their performance.

Collaborate with school staff, central office, and local board of education regarding the school improvement plan and make recommendations as the plan is implemented.

Report to the local board of education, the community, and the state board of education regarding the school's progress.

Empower the staff to continue the school improvement process in the future (team building strategies).

Solicit feedback and suggestions routinely.

Assist the school in identifying, locating, and gathering resources that support a strong instructional program.

Update the school on a regular basis concerning all aspects of the school improvement process.

Here are some ways to describe the helping relationship of school assistance teams.

We are an extension of the school staff whose purpose is to improve student performance.

We don't have all the answers but believe that you have the answers and that our role is to help you focus and channel your expertise and energy.

We believe that by working together, we will be successful in meeting the school improvement plan goals.

ARTIFACT 9. STATE ASSISTANCE TEAM CLASSROOM MONITORING INSTRUMENT

*Teacher*_____ *Date*_____ *Time*_____

*Subject*_____ *Grade*_____ *Observer*_____

LESSON PLAN: _____Yes _____No

Objective: _____

Activity: _____

Instructional Strategies:	Student Activities:	Materials/ Equipment:
___Cooperative Learning	___Games	___Computers
___Small Group	___Drill/Practice	___Chalkboard
___Large Group	___Guided Practice	___Overhead
___Resource Person	___Learning Contracts	___AV Usage
___Student Presentation	___Role-Playing	___Manipulatives
___Teacher Demonstration	___Projects	
___Coaching	___Oral Reading	*Assessment:*
___Lecture	___Written Activities	___Tests
___Peer Tutoring	___Textbooks	___Homework
___Higher-Order Questioning	___Worksheets	___Lesson Closure
___Teacher Assistant Involved	___Student Presentation	
___Centers		
___Research		
___Silent Reading		

Classroom Management: ___Well Established ___Somewhat Established ___Not Established

Comments/Suggestions: _____

_____

_____

_____

ARTIFACT 10. SUPERINTENDENT'S REPORT TO THE PINEVILLE SCHOOL BOARD

As the board will remember, all school systems in the state are now at the end of year two of a state-mandated accountability process. The name given to the overall process is the School Excellence Plan (SEP). To this point, only elementary and secondary schools have been participating. Next year, high schools will enter the SEP process. For an overview of the key features of the state plan, please refer to Attachment 1.

Recently, several implications of this accountability process were brought forcibly to our attention when we received the state's analysis of the achievement of our elementary and middle school students as measured against what they should have achieved. As specified in the SEP legislation, our test scores were published in the local paper, along with the scores of neighboring school systems. In general, Pineville students did not fare well on the tests, and two elementary schools in particular were given "low-performing status." At present, a state assistance team is working with the Green Valley Elementary and Washington Elementary Schools. Our experience at these schools points up a larger agenda for the Pineville Schools: What must we do to restore our historical reputation as a school system of excellence for all children?

Our SEP performance has produced expressions of concern, frustration, and questions from teachers, administrators, the community, and members of the school board. My report tonight is in response to these concerns and specifically responds to the charge given me at the last board meeting to bring a proposal that "addresses the current achievement scores and plans to improve student achievement across the board."

Before sharing my plan, I'd like to describe the planning process we engaged in to gather as much pertinent data as possible. First, I met with the central office staff, a group of professionals having a wealth of educational expertise. Next, I met with the building-level administrators who were asked to consult with their faculties before the meeting, consistent with our site-based management philosophy. Finally, I arranged three open meetings with the public. There was a meeting that targeted the parents of elementary students and children soon to enter our schools. A second meeting was held for recognized community leaders; the final open meeting was for business people as well as parents and other interested citizens.

As we analyzed the problem from the viewpoint of educators, several conclusions emerged:

1. Successful education is the result of a long-term process, but it must focus on a student's earlier schooling experience to be successful.
2. Consistent with this, we must place a disproportionate share of our resources at the front end of our formal instructional process. Our students exceed state testing standards at the high school level, but many come to us with seriously delayed development and are unprepared for the requirements of formal schooling.
3. Given this philosophy, we concluded that if we concentrated on grades K–3, and if we focused on two schools (Green Valley and Washington) as centers for front loading, we could concentrate our district's instructional resources in a more effective fashion.

After a great deal of discussion, our building-level administrators reached consensus in support of the front-loading concept. Next, we held meetings with the various segments of our community as mentioned previously. Here is a summary of the outcomes of this process.

1. Many parents of the children targeted to attend Green Valley and Washington Schools were appreciative of the special assistance and increased allocation of resources their children would receive.
2. If these two schools became centers for those students who had not reached acceptable achievement levels, they would house most of the district's K–3 minority student population. Some white parents were concerned that this might encourage another wave of "white flight." Some black parents, on the other hand, were concerned that these two school centers may negatively affect the self-esteem of the students who attend. Both black and white parents expressed concern that this would, in effect, create two segregated schools.
3. Another concern voiced was the long-term impact a heavy front-loading of instructional resources would have on the funding of other schools in the system, as well as on those grade levels after Grade 3.

You can see that there are concerns about the front-loading concept. But there are many who strongly advocate this idea as well. I am convinced that in spite of some legitimate concerns, the idea will be successful and over time, the achievement levels of all our students will be positively impacted.

Therefore, I recommend that the board adopt the front-loading proposal. If the board concurs, I have a funding plan prepared for your consideration.

In addition, I propose the following system-wide strategies to improve student achievement across the board.

1. All instruction will be aligned with the state's standard curriculum in terms of content, its scope, and its sequence.
2. Teachers will be required to complete a set of specific instructional objectives each quarter and test student achievement levels in a format consistent with the state's end-of-course tests.
3. Teachers will receive in-service training on diverse student learning styles and how to appropriately provide instruction that addresses these.
4. The school system will first determine what are the essential instructional resources that must be found in each classroom and then determine what resources are actually available in each school. Steps will be taken to redress any inequities. Each school will be responsible for making sure every classroom has the essential resources for instructional support.
5. We will establish an Administrator Academy for Pineville City Schools designed to assist building-level administrators to become instructional leaders in their schools.

6. A position of Literacy Specialist will be added to the staff of each elementary and middle school to assist classroom teachers in their efforts to produce higher levels of student literacy.

7. Finally, because the SEP places primary instructional accountability squarely with the individual school, we will review our district's site-based management plan to determine what is the appropriate division of rules, roles, and relationships between schools and the central administration within the state's accountability framework. While affirming the value of site-based management, let us remember that we have a Pineville school system, not a system of Pineville schools.

I believe this report responds appropriately to the board's charge. I also believe that if the recommendations contained in the report receive the endorsement of the board, the future achievement levels of all our students will be greatly improved.

ARTIFACT 11. SUPERINTENDENT'S REPORT, ATTACHMENT 1: THE SCHOOL EXCELLENCE PLAN

Three years ago, the State Legislature directed the State Board of Education to craft a plan that reorganizes public education within the state. This plan became known as the School Excellence Plan or SEP. Under this plan local school districts are provided both the authority and the accountability to succeed. Previously, educational reform initiatives focused on input. This plan is different because it focuses on results—what the student has learned in the most important academic areas. And for the first time, schools will have the flexibility to do what they believe will help them achieve high performance standards. But also, for the first time, schools must meet performance standards or outside caretakers will be appointed to fix the problems.

The State Board of Education's plan emphasizes strong accountability, a focus on the basics, maximum local control and flexibility, and high educational standards.

Accountability: Strong accountability means that if a local school performs well, it will be eligible for bonus rewards from the state. If a local school does not meet performance standards, the State Board will send an assistance team to recommend changes. If more than one-half of the schools in a district fail to meet standards, the State Board will appoint a caretaker superintendent, and teacher tenure for the schools not meeting standards will be suspended. Local authority and tenure will be restored when the local district begins achieving standards.

Basics: Grades 3–8 will use the end-of-grade tests in reading, writing (grades 4 and 7), and mathematics. Grades 4–8 will use the previous end-of-grade tests as a pre-test. A pre-test will be given at the start of the third grade since there is no end-of-grade test in the second grade.

Performance Growth Standards: At least a year's worth of growth for a year's worth of schooling will be expected. The SEP is based on performance at the individual school level rather than the school district level. School growth will be the expected growth rate for that school based on previous performance statewide. Exemplary growth will be 110 percent of the expected growth rate. Growth standards will take into account the difficulty of already high performing schools attempting to make large gains. The State Board will not impose the method to achieve high educational standards, but will insist that high standards be attained.

School Incentive Awards: Based on growth standards, all schools will have the opportunity to receive awards. Awards will be allocated based on the number of certified staff at the school. The certified staff will vote on the use of the funds.

Recognition: A recognition program that acknowledges exemplary performance will be developed by the State Board of Education.

Assistance: There are two types of state assistance: 1) voluntary assistance for schools that request it; and 2) assistance for those schools that fail to meet their expected growth standard and have a high number of students performing below grade level proficiency. These schools will automatically be eligible for assistance. Voluntary assistance will be provided, as much as possible, to any school system that requests help. These assistance teams will be comprised of educators and others selected by the State Board of Education for their expertise and successful track record.

Intervention: State intervention could occur at any time but is anticipated to occur after assistance efforts have not resulted in improvement. Naming a replacement principal would be a culminating event that occurs only after all assistance has failed to produce results. Board members make it clear that they did not want to be in a position of having to take over schools. At the same time, they feel responsible for students who are in schools that are getting worse over time and that are already low performing.

Under SEP, school systems will have more control over how to spend state education dollars and how to educate their own students. This will give schools the opportunity to develop innovative programs tailored to meet the needs of their students. Parents, employers, and prospective businesses must regain confidence in the schools of our state. The SEP offers the best opportunity for that to happen.

Index

Louisville, Kentucky, 50
low academic achievement, 56
low performing designation, 15
low performing school, 14

Mankiewicz, Frank, 62
March, Victoria, 154, 156, 157
Mariposa Unified School District
    (MUSD), composition of, 152
Marshall, Stephanie Pace, principal of
    IMSA, 51
Martin, Don, 42, 43, 44, 45, 46, 47, 49,
    50, 60
McKensie Company, 157
media hostility, 61
media representation, political ramification
    of, 61
media scrutiny, 93
media/press, negative slant of, 62
meeting with faculty, staff, and parents of
    two schools, 15
merit pay, 151, 152, 153, 154, 155, 156,
    157
merit pay system, 8, 25
micro-management, 49, 120, 135
minority students, 110
mission statement, 81, 125
Morris, Buddy, 121, 122, 123, 124;
    adjustments in his routine, 127
Mr.: English, Mr. Art, and Mr. Mathe-
    matics (Mr. Eam), 33, 35, 36, 38;
    Foreign (Language), 33, 34, 36, 37;
    History, 33, 34, 35, 36; PE, 33, 35,
    36, 38
multi-disciplinary approach, 89
myth of apolitical schools, 85

NAACP, 10, 18
Nation at Risk, A, 28
National Merit scholars, 30, 106, 111
national reputation, 25
National Superintendent of the Year, 103
nature and effects of power relationships,
    61
NEA, 15
new curriculum, 6, 81
new-generational thinking, 47, 54, 59

Newspaper, 62, 63, 64, 65, 66, 67, 68,
    71, 73, 74, 75, 76, 77, 79; abusive
    behavior of, 65, 66; attitude of Kelly
    towards, 72, 73; editorials of, 63, 64;
    focus on negative and sensational, 65,
    66; lack of objectivity, 64, 65, 68, 69;
    misrepresenting the school district,
    65, 66; opening superintendent's
    mail, 74; personal attacks by, 63, 66,
    67; quoting out of context/miscon-
    struing facts, 64, 67; strategy for
    dealing with, 72, 73, 74; support for
    previous superintendent, 68, 69
notion of leadership and learning, 52
notion of power, 6

organizational change and school
    community relations, 7
Outcomes-Based Education (OBE), 137
Outcomes-Based Education (OBE) grant,
    136, 144
Outlook, 11
outside consultant, 127
Oxford, 35

Paine, Jim, 111, 112, 113, 115, 116
Palmer, J. M., 85
Parent Action Team, 126
parent group, 7
parents as an organized force, 15
Parker, 151
participatory decision making, 57
peer coaching, 47
perception of principal, 122
perceptions of teachers, self-perceptions,
    128
performance goals, 112
personnel office, 26
Peterson, Marion, 30, 31
Phi Delta Kappan, 147
philosophy of inclusive action, 80
Pineville, 10, 11, 12, 14, 15, 16, 17, 19;
    city schools, 10; schools SEP test
    scores, chart, 14
planning committee, 108
planning wheel, 86, 87
*Planning Wheels Turn Curriculum
    Around,* 85

student-centered approach, 46
student-centered instruction, 139, 140, 141
students: attitudes of, 91; as knowledge providers, 58; as learners and teachers, 58; as passive recipients of knowledge, 58
Students Speak: How Kentucky Middle and High School Students View Schools, 57
succession as a factor of superintendent affectiveness, 6, 44
summer library program, 17
Sunshine Laws, 63, 72, 74; definition of, 63
superintendency, political nature of, 7
superintendent: ability to work with others, 70, 71; balance between professional and personal life, 7; contract negotiations, 66; definition of power, 72, 78; empowerment of faculty, 42, 49; evaluation of the school district, 100; experience, 11; involvement in the community, 74; issues facing, 6, 8; leadership/ management style, 6, 7, 8, 25, 118; mistakes of predecessor impacting current goals/objectives, 69, 77; necessity of political acuity and communication skills, 43; qualities, 43; relationship with media, 6, 7; relationship with school board, 6, 8; relationship with school board, parents, and community members, 6; reputation of, 111, 25, 32; use of power, 7, 71
Superintendent of the Year, 66, 147; competition, 60
superintendent selection committee, 23, 31
superintendent selection process, 120
support of school-site instructional improvement, 133
Support Staff Action Team, 126
survey of students' preferences, 58
system of education, 43

Talk of the Town, 144
targeted for "takeover," 15

task force, 53
tax for new schools, 67
teacher: and administrator relationships, 55; attitude of toward curriculum, 88; isolation of, 121; resistance to change from, 88; role of, 55; and student relationships, 55; of the year, 48
teaching and learning, 28, 29, 31, 36
team approach, 70
team building, 125, 126
team collaboration, 100
team leadership, definition of, 46
team management system, 32
team performance and collaboration, 124
teamwork culture, 100
Tellerico and Burnstyn, 2
territorial attitudes among staff and students, 37
test performance by students, 111; reported to the public, 13
test scores, 10, 15, 105, 113, 114; affect of on staff, 15; compared with those of the other school systems in the area, 10; declining, 1; effect by developmentally delayed students 17; effect on businesses, 11; as evidence of good schools, 11; SAT and ACT, 52, 107, 111, 113; SEP, compared with other area school districts, 14
tests: as mechanisms of evaluation, 9; national and state, 11
Texas Education Agency, 106
Times Outlook newspaper, 10
total enrollment in the classroom, 17
total minority population, 16
track record, 31
traditional notion of the structure of school, 56
traditional school practice, 141
transformational and instructional leaders, 2
Transformations, 49
tuition paying transfer students, 12
type of district, 11

unanimous vote by board regarding superintendent appointment, 45

About the Contributors

Paula M. Short is associate vice president for academic affairs at the University of Missouri System. She has a Ph.D. in educational administration from the University of North Carolina at Chapel Hill. She was formerly chair of the department of Educational Leadership and Policy Analysis at the University of Missouri–Columbia and served on the faculty at the Pennsylvania State University. Her research interests include the superintendency, empowerment, organizational change, leadership, and collaboration in higher education. She received the Jack Culbertson Award in 1993, given nationally to a professor in the first ten years in academe, for excellence in research in educational administration. Recent publications include *Leadership in Empowered Schools: Themes From Innovative Efforts* (with Jack Greer), "Reflection in Leader Preparation" in the *Peabody Journal of Education*, and "Empowering Leadership" in *Contemporary Education*. She has served as president of the University Council for Educational Administration, Southern Regional Council for Educational Administration, and the National Council of Professors of Educational Administration.

Jay Paredes Scribner is assistant professor in the department of Educational Leadership and Policy Analysis at the University of Missouri–Columbia. He received his Ph.D. in educational administration from the University of Wisconsin–Madison in 1997. His research focuses on formal and informal teacher learning, organizational learning, leadership, and program evaluation in education. Recent publications include "Inter-Organizational Collaboration in a Statewide Doctoral Program" (with J. Machell) in the *Journal of School Leadership*, "Framing Professional Development" in the *Journal of Staff Development*, "Teacher Efficacy and Teacher Professional

Learning: Implications for School Leaders" in the *Journal of School Leadership,* and "Professional Development: Untangling the Influence of Work Context on Teacher Learning" in *Educational Administration Quarterly.* His dissertation, "Exploring the Context of Teacher Work and Professional Development in Urban High Schools," won the 1998 Best Dissertation Research award from the National Staff Development Council.

THE CONTRIBUTORS

Carl R. Ashbaugh is a professor of educational administration at the University of North Carolina–Charlotte. During a career that spans forty-five years, he has also served as a public school teacher, administrator, and dean of education. His research interests are school organization, school change and improvement, and reforming school administrator preparation programs. Recently, the latter interest has been expressed through research that focuses on student portfolios, case study instruction, and the administrative internship. His most recent publication with relevance to this book is *Educational Leadership: Case Studies for Reflective Practice* (with Katherine L. Kasten).

Judith H. Berg is an associate professor in the Division of Educational Leadership and Policy Studies at the University of Northern Colorado. With a focused interest in leadership at the district level, specifically politics and the superintendent of schools, Judith's research and other scholarly pursuits over the last several years have been focused by leadership efforts at the district level, most particularly the political work of the superintendent of schools, and collaborative efforts between districts and other youth and family serving agencies. Recent publications with this focus include "A Typology of Partnerships for Promoting Innovation" in *The Journal of School Leadership* (Nov. 1999, with B. Barnett, G. Hall, and M. Camarena), "The School District Superintendent: Attention Must Be Paid" in *The AASA Professor* (Winter/Spring 1999, with B. Barnett), and "Intersection of Political Leadership and Educational Excellence: A Neglected Leadership Domain" in *The AASA Professor* (Summer 1999, with G. E. Hall). Judith serves as a reviewer for the *Journal of School Leadership,* a Plenum representative for the university to the University Council of Educational Administration. She has served as program and membership chairperson for the AERA SIG Research on the Superintendency, and is a member of the Northern Colorado Superintendents Council. She was a member of a small group of selected scholars who conceptualized and implemented UCEA's "Voices from the Firing Line" project (a study of superintendents' working conditions and their perceptions of their preparation programs). Currently she is engaged in a collaborative research effort with a superintendent of schools.

Lars G. Björk joined the University of Kentucky faculty in January 1996. He is the co-director of the University Council for Educational Administration's joint Program Center for the Study of the Superintendency and is a senior associate editor of *Educational Administration Quarterly*. Dr. Björk has co-edited *Higher Education Research and Public Policy* (1988) and *Minorities in Higher Education* (1994). In addition he is co-author of *The Study of the American Superintendency: 2000* (with Thomas Glass and C. Cryss Brunner) and is co-editing *The New Superintendency* (with C. Cryss Brunner), which will be released by JAI Press in 2001. His previous experience includes serving on the faculties of the Georgia Southern University, University of South Carolina, and the University of New Mexico. In addition he has served as Executive Assistant to the Director of the National Institute of Education, as a senior staff member of Westinghouse Learning Corporation, and as Regional Director for University Research Corporation. In addition to serving as a consultant to institutions of higher education, school districts, state governments, and international agencies, he has been a member of advisory, coordinating committees, and task forces in the U.S. Department of Education. Dr. Björk holds a Ph.D. and an Ed.S. in educational administration, an M.Ed. in public administration, an M.Ed. in secondary education, and a B.A. in education from the University of New Mexico. His areas of academic interest and expertise include the superintendency, organizational change, school reform, organizational theory, school-university collaboration, and qualitative research methodology.

C. Cryss Brunner is an assistant professor in the department of educational administration at the University of Wisconsin–Madison. She completed her Ph.D. at the University of Kansas in 1993. Her research on women, power, the superintendency, and the gap between public schools and their communities has appeared in such journals as *Educational Policy, Journal for a Just and Caring Education, Policy Studies Journal, The School Administrator, Educational Considerations, Contemporary Education,* and *The Journal of School Leadership*. State University of New York Press published her edited book *Sacred Dreams: Women and the Superintendency* (1999) and her book *Principles of Power: Women Superintendents and the Riddle of the Heart* (forthcoming). Brunner is the 1996–97 recipient of the National Academy of Education's Spencer Fellowship for her work on the relationship between superintendents' definitions of power and decision-making processes. She is the 1998 recipient of the University Council for Educational Administration's Jack Culbertson Award for her outstanding contributions to the field of educational administration. In addition, she serves as joint director of the UCEA Joint Program Center for the Study of the Superintendency.

William G. Cunningham is professor of educational leadership at Old Dominion University in Norfolk, Virginia. He earned his B.A. degree (1964) in industrial technology and management at Miami University and his Ph.D. degree (1974) in educational administration and research at Duke University. He has served in various roles in both business and education. His main research focus has been on leadership, planning, and continuous educational improvement. He is an innovative consultant; has made over one hundred presentations at national, state, and local conferences; published widely in educational journals; and is often interviewed for the print media and radio. His most recent books are *Educational Administration: A Problem-Based Approach* with P. A. Corediro, *The American School Superintendent: Leading in an Age of Pressure* with G. R. Carter and W. G. Cunningham, *Cultured Leadership: The Culture of Excellence in Education* with W. G. Cunningham and D. W. Gresso.

Nadyne Guzmán is an associate professor at the University of Colorado at Colorado Springs and program coordinator of educational leadership. Dr. Guzmán came to the university in 1991 after fifteen years in K–12 education as a teacher and administrator. The major focus of her research is the process of collaborative leadership within the development of learning communities, and the human element within that process. Her research has been presented at major research conferences and her work has been published in a variety of publications including *Journal of Leadership Studies, CAPEA Journal, Journal of Educational Administration*, and *Planning and Changing*. She has also collaborated in the development of and instruction in an inter-campus Ph.D. program and an undergraduate leadership development program. Dr. Guzmán has also served as a change process, planning, and curriculum consultant for various public and private schools and districts as well as Fortune 500 companies.

Cheryl Holder has been the director of special education services for Scottsboro City Schools, Scottsboro, Alabama, since 1990. In addition to those duties, she has also served as the system Title IV, Title IX, 504, and ADA Coordinator, Staff Development Coordinator, School Health Services Coordinator, and Counseling Coordinator. Prior to her current supervisory position, Cheryl had experience as a school system psychometrist, special education teacher, and mental health worker on a special project for the Alabama State Department of Education, assisting in implementation of a new diploma option for students with disabilities.

John R. Hoyle is professor of educational administration at Texas A&M University. His research interests include leadership roles of superintendents and principals, future schools, leadership and visioning, and the power of hope and love on school improvement. He is an international consultant and speaker for business, agriculture, and education. He served as chair of the American Association of School Administrator's National Commission on Standards for the Superintendency and President of NCPEA. He received the first "living legend" award at the 1999 National Conference of Professors of Educational Administration. Recent publications include "The Politics of Superintendent Evaluation" in the *Journal of Personnel Evaluation in Education* (with Linda Skrla), *Skills for Successful 21st Century School Leaders* (with Fenwick English and Betty Steffy); and *Leadership and Futuring: Making Visions Happen.*

Patsy Johnson is associate professor of educational leadership at the University of Connecticut. She has her doctorate in educational leadership from Auburn University. Her research interests include conflict management, school-based reform, and site-based management. Patsy serves as a consultant to schools and school districts around the country on change and conflict management. For her dissertation, she received the Outstanding Dissertation Award from the National Council of Professors of Educational Administration. She also has received the Jack Culbertson Award from UCEA for outstanding contributions to research in educational administration.

John L. Keedy, a former principal and assistant superintendent, is now an associate professor in the Department of Administration and Higher Education at the University of Louisville. His research interests are in school reform, conceptual frameworks of school reform players, and school norms. He has published in the *Journal of Curriculum Studies, Theory Into Practice, The Journal of School Leadership*, and the *Journal of Educational Research*, among others. He is beginning a study of school councils in Kentucky.

Mary Gonzales Mend is the superintendent of the American School Foundation; a private K–12 college preparatory located in Mexico City. Virtually 100 percent of ASF graduates attend a college or university. Much of her career has been in California public school district administration. She seeks to inform practice through collaborative research on politics and organizational effectiveness.

Ann G. Mullin is an education specialist with the Department of Correction, State of North Carolina. She has a Ph.D. in educational leadership and program evaluation from North Carolina State University. Her experience includes twenty-five years of teaching and administration in public, private, and parochial education. Her research interests focus on transformational leadership behaviors and the effects of those behaviors on the change process at all levels of public education.

Flora Ida Ortiz specializes in socialization processes, educational administration careers, and educational facilities planning and designing. She has written extensively in each area. Most recently, she has addressed the issue of Hispanic female superintendents and their success.

Al Ramirez is an associate professor in the Educational Leadership program at the University of Colorado at Colorado Springs. His recent transition to university level teaching follows a twenty-five year career in pre-K through 14 education. Al's experience includes positions as a teacher, counselor, principal, central office administrator, and superintendent of schools. He has also held key educational policy positions in the Nevada and Illinois State Departments of Education and served in the role of chief state school officer in Iowa. Al has published widely on a variety of education topics in such journals as *Kappan, Executive Educator, Educational Leadership,* and *The American School Board Journal,* and he has presented at numerous state, national, and international education conferences. Al also served appointments to several national education advisory boards and commissions. Al's consulting work has a client list that includes Arthur Andersen's School of the Future, several large urban school districts, and the U.S. Department of Education.